PUPPET PLANET

John E. Kennedy

NORTH LIGHT BOOKS
CINCINNATI, OHIO
www.artistsnetwork.com

WITHDRAWN

10 09 08 07 06   5 4 3 2 1

Distributed in Canada by Fraser Direct
100 Armstrong Avenue
Georgetown, ON, Canada L7G 5S4
Tel: (905) 877-4411

Distributed in the U.K. and Europe by David & Charles
Brunel House, Newton Abbot, Devon, TQ12 4PU, England
Tel: (+44) 1626 323200, Fax: (+44) 1626 323319
E-mail: mail@davidandcharles.co.uk

Distributed in Australia by Capricorn Link
P.O. Box 704, S. Windsor, NSW 2756 Australia
Tel: (02) 4577-3555

Library of Congress Cataloging-in-Publication Data

Kennedy, John E.
   Puppet planet : the best puppet-making book in the universe /
John E. Kennedy. -- 1st ed.
      p. cm.
   Includes index.
   ISBN-13: 978-1-58180-794-3 (pbk. : alk. paper)
   ISBN-10: 1-58180-794-5
   1. Puppet making.   I. Title.
TT174.7.K47 2006
745.592'24--dc22
                                    2005033711

Foaman and The Foaman Empire are trademarks of John E. Kennedy

United States Patent
Kennedy
US 6,540,581 B2
April 1, 2003
Puppet Construction Kit and method of
making a personalized hand operated puppet.

Metric Conversion Chart

TO CONVERT	TO	MULTIPLY BY
Inches	Centimeters	2.54
Centimeters	Inches	0.4
Feet	Centimeters	30.5
Centimeters	Feet	0.03
Yards	Meters	0.9
Meters	Yards	1.1
Sq. Inches	Sq. Centimeters	6.45
Sq. Centimeters	Sq. Inches	0.16
Sq. Feet	Sq. Meters	0.09
Sq. Meters	Sq. Feet	10.8
Sq. Yards	Sq. Meters	0.8
Sq. Meters	Sq. Yards	1.2
Pounds	Kilograms	0.45
Kilograms	Pounds	2.2
Ounces	Grams	28.4
Grams	Ounces	0.04

Editor: David Oeters
Designer: Terri Eubanks
      and Marissa Bowers
Cover Designers: Leigh Ann Lentz
      and Marissa Bowers
Layout Artist: Kathy Gardner
Production Coordinator: Greg Nock
Photographers: Christine Polomsky,
      Tim Grondin, Al Parrish
      and Harvey Smith
Photo Stylist: Jan Nickum

F+W PUBLICATIONS, INC.

About the author

John E. Kennedy has worked with The Jim Henson Company for more than fifteen years and has also worked in "The Muppet Revue" at Walt Disney World, where he spent time working directly with Jim Henson. John has taught puppet making to children at museum workshops and has worked on "Sesame Street," "The Wubbulous World of Dr. Seuss," "Muppets from Space," "The Muppets' Wizard of Oz," "Animal Jam" and "Jack's Big Music Show." He travels extensively for film work and has been a frequent guest on HGTV's "Carol Duvall Show." John is currently teaching a graduate-level course on puppetry at the University of Central Florida. He lives in Ocoee, Florida, with his wife, Julie.

Acknowledgments

I want to thank some key people in my life who believed in me and encouraged me to be the best I could be.

Thanks to . . .
Peter D. Sims, my high school choir director,
for helping me find the entertainer in me;

my college mentor, Dr. Dorothy Webb, for designing
a puppet program just for me;

Verna Finly, for teaching me her craft;

and Jane Henson, for inviting me to her workshop.

Each of you have brought me creative inspiration and
a creative place to draw from within myself.

Dedication

THIS BOOK IS DEDICATED TO EVERYONE WHO DARES TO BE DIFFERENT. IT TAKES COURAGE TO STAND UP FOR YOUR OWN THOUGHTS AND IDEAS, AND A LOT OF DETERMINATION TO SEE THEM THROUGH. IF ONE NEW CHARACTER IS BORN FROM THIS BOOK, I'LL CONSIDER IT A SUCCESS.

Finding Your Way on Puppet Planet

Welcome to Puppet Planet

My best friend, Ed Lucas, and I got our first job performing puppets at the Elks Club in Plainfield, Indiana. We continued to land more gigs after that show. Ed's dad built an amazing, wooden stage that came in pretty handy because, before long, we were all over town doing parties and special events. Back then we weren't sure what we were doing, but we kept working to fulfill our dreams of entertaining people. That was my first experience on what I've come to call Puppet Planet.

Welcome to Puppet Planet, the place where puppet dreams can become reality! What you hold in your hand is what I consider to be the very first guidebook to puppetry. Its purpose is to provide you with a blueprint for creating new characters, methods for honing your performance skills, and help you discover the wonderful experiences waiting for you on Puppet Planet. While traveling on this planet, you'll discover a new civilization of wonderful creatures and a world where everyone is free to express themselves and have fun doing so. You are encouraged to discover your artistic side and, just as Ed and I did as sixth graders, get out and share your talents.

Don't worry; we're not going to let you get lost on Puppet Planet. This guidebook is filled with tips, techniques and ideas. You'll find field guide pages that give you an in-depth look at the citizens of Puppet Planet and how to use them outside of your workshop. You'll also meet Professor Foaman, the smartest puppet on Puppet Planet (or so he believes), who will be your mentor. His experiments and studies in puppet building have given him a bevy of useful travel tips for anyone visiting the planet.

Intrigued yet? I'm going to let you in on a little secret—Puppet Planet isn't really a location, but a new way of thinking. Like a puppeteer, you're going to start looking for creative inspiration everywhere. You won't need a passport to visit this planet. All you need is a willingness to have fun and to be open to a creative vision, and you're there.

Ed and I still talk about our journey as young puppeteers, and the characters we created continue hold a special place in our hearts. The memories and positive values I gained during that time have influenced my entire life. Puppet Planet isn't just about making puppets, but about entertaining, performing and exploring your own creative vision. It's about having confidence in your own ability and being open to new ideas. It's about having fun. I hope your time on Puppet Planet will be as amazing as mine.

John Kennedy

An Insider's Guide to Tools

Basic Tools

When exploring Puppet Planet, it's important to have the proper tools to get the job done safely and right. You want the audience to see that your puppets are made with love and respect for the art of puppetry. I suggest going through the list below, checking off the tools you already have and finding those that you'll need. Once you have a good set of tools, organize them in something easy to carry around so you'll be prepared when inspiration strikes.

Scissors

Assemble a collection of scissors for different purposes. Don't cut fabric and plastic with the same scissors. Save your fabric scissors for cutting fabric, and they will stay sharp longer.

Needle-nose pliers

You'll find needle-nose pliers at any hardware store. The needle-nose is great for clamping down and holding hard-to-reach materials, and pulling the tip of a needle through fabric when you're sewing. Look for pliers with a wire cutter so you can cut and bend wires with the same tool.

Permanent ink marker

I use a permanent ink marker to trace patterns on paper, fabric and plastic because it doesn't rub off on your fingers. The markers come in a wide variety of colors so you can use them to put finishing touches on your puppets. For a unique effect, use a little rubbing alcohol with an applicator sponge to blend colors on foam rubber or fabrics.

Ruler

Your puppet will look more professional if it has symmetry. Use a ruler for tracing straight lines and measuring. Use a measuring tape for getting accurate measurements around angles and shapes.

Paintbrush

I use a paintbrush for paints that I can wash out. For all other paints and glues I use a foam brush because they are generally disposable. A foam brush is especially good at painting foam rubber.

Hole punch

A hole punch is safer to use than a drill. It makes a clean hole in cardboard and plastic. You can also create holes to lace things together with string. Try using a hole punch on black plastic or cardboard to make pupils for eyes.

Glue

You can find many different kinds of glue at your local craft stores. Read the labels to learn how to best use different types of glue. Find a glue that works for the surfaces you are using. For many of these projects, I use hot glue. It secures quickly and easily. See page 9 for more safety tips when using a glue gun.

Contact cement

Contact cement is available at hardware stores and some grocery stores. It works quickly and holds tightly. I use a foam wedge to apply contact cement to both sides of what I want glued, then press the surfaces together. Work in a well-ventilated area, and keep the cement away from your skin.

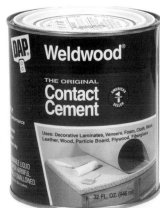

Cable ties

Drill or punch holes in your materials and lash them together with cable ties, which can be found at hardware stores. Then you won't need to use messy glue.

Drill

Nothing makes a better hole in some materials than a drill. If you can, use a vise to secure the material. If a vise isn't available, then make sure you're drilling on a flat, protected surface. A Dremel is a rotary tool that can also be used as a drill, and can be found at your local hardware store. See page 14 for more information on using a Dremel to smooth foam.

Electric carving knife

This useful foam-carving tool is hard to find except around Thanksgiving. I try to find electric knives with long blades because you don't want to stifle your creativity by only being able to cut thin pieces of foam. Be careful using the electric knife. What can carve a turkey can also carve your skin.

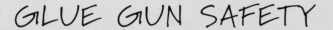

GLUE GUN SAFETY

Be very careful when using a glue gun. Hot glue can burn your skin and be a fire hazard. Before using a hot glue gun, take a look at your project. A glue gun can quickly and efficiently assemble a puppet, but other forms of glue might work safer and more efficiently than hot glue. Sewing is often the best option.

When you use hot glue, remember to follow some basic safety tips:

✤ Before starting, take time to decide where you need glue and how much is needed. Be aware of any hazards in the area you are gluing, such as fur that will stick together or plastic that might melt.

✤ Apply a small bead of glue instead of a big bubble since the center of a bubble takes more time to cool. Don't touch it right away; you may think the glue is cool, but the center will still be hot.

✤ Be careful where you leave a hot glue gun. Place it on a heat-resistant surface when you're not using it to avoid melting or burning. Never leave it unattended while it's plugged in. A hot glue gun will remain hot for some time after it's unplugged.

An Insider's Guide to Materials

Basic Materials

You may be surprised to learn that finding the right materials for puppets can be tricky. My search often takes me on unexpected adventures. How do you tell a store clerk that you intend to make wolf eyebrows with the fur trim of a tube top you saw in an advertisement? Don't worry; you'll think of something. That's what a visionary shopper does. A visionary shopper is able to see puppets everywhere. You'll build characters in your mind from items you see as you shop, such as a bicycle horn that can be a nose. List where you can find these materials in your area, so you aren't constantly searching instead of creating.

Fake fur

Fur comes in a variety of colors and two types: long shag and short shag. Long shag fake fur is great for making hair. Short shag fur is useful for puppet skin, and it hides seams well. Most fabric stores carry fur, but it's easiest to find in colder seasons.

Felt

Felt can be used to make puppet clothes, mouth linings, tongues and so much more. You can also wet and shape felt, and it will hold its shape. This versatile fabric can be found in craft or fabric stores.

Sheet foam

Sheet foam can be found at craft stores and some fabric stores. This is another one of those multipurpose materials. You can paint it, glue it and make teeth and eyes out of it, among other things.

Soft foam rubber

This foam is soft and flexible and primarily used in bedding and packing, but also makes an excellent material for puppets. See page 11 for information on finding foam. I use 1" (3cm) and 5" (13cm) foam in this book. Never expose foam to fire or a hot surface.

Stuffing

I use stuffing, also known as batting, to fill out patterned shapes that don't need to have a strong structure. A tail, ears or floppy arms can be stuffed in seconds. Fabric and craft stores stock stuffing.

Acrylic paint

Acrylic paint is a common craft store item and is great for puppet making. You can color foam, paper or other items with acrylic paint, or add it to latex rubber as a colorant.

Pom-poms

Eyes, teeth, noses and accents are some of the many uses for pom-poms. They come in all sizes and colors at the craft store and can be easily applied to a puppet with glue.

Puppet eyes

Bubble circles are clear plastic stickers that can be used to make eyes. They can be found wherever scrapbook supplies are sold. Clasp eyes are used in dollmaking and are excellent puppet eyes. They are becoming more difficult to find, but I've still been able to buy them from specialty craft stores.

Needle and thread

I have a collection of sewing needles—super long ones, curved ones, ones with bigger eyes and really sharp ones. It takes a thick thread or fishing line to get the kind of durability you need with puppets. A sewing machine is faster and sometimes more effective than hand sewing.

Polymer clay

Polymer clay is great for making a rough model of a character idea before you begin. Polymer clay is also good for making molds. Sculpt a puppet nose, cast it in plaster and pull out the clay. The mold is instantly ready for coating with latex.

Plaster

Plaster comes in a variety of consistencies. I like a more rigid mix of plaster because it will hold the details of a sculpture better. Be careful not to pour excess plaster down a drain because it will harden in the pipes and cause a plaster plumbing disaster.

Latex rubber

Latex rubber is a wonderful material for making realistic puppet parts. Work in a well-ventilated area and wear old clothes because latex won't wash out. I normally work with latex in what's known as a "slush mold technique." With this technique you sculpt something out of clay, cast it in plaster and remove the clay, then slush the latex into the mold. See the Monkey Mitten project on page 46 for more information on using latex.

FINDING FOAM

Finding a supplier for certain materials wherever I happen to be has become a mental game. I've lived in many different places and I have a library of puppet supply stores around the country.

Foam rubber can be hard to find, but the first step is to check the local phone book for upholstery shops and fabric stores, where you can often find many different types of foam. When I build puppets like Foaman, I use bedding foam. This is a soft, white foam rubber that comes in a variety of thicknesses and is usually the size of a double bed mattress. If I don't need much foam, I'll use pillow foam. Another great place to find foam is a packing company. They specialize in cutting and shaping a wide variety of foam styles and colors, and will often just throw away scraps that puppeteers can use. I didn't know I had so many foam choices until I visited a local packing plant.

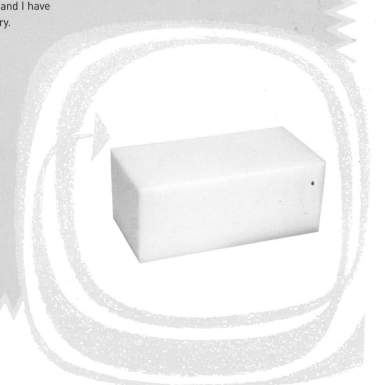

An Insider's Guide to Techniques

Using Patterns

Tracing and cutting out patterns is an important part of building a professional-looking puppet. A mistake can leave you with pieces that don't fit or a puppet that doesn't work. For the best results, label your patterns, and slowly trace and cut out each piece.

Preparing the pattern

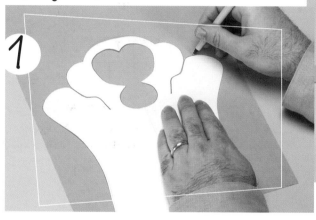

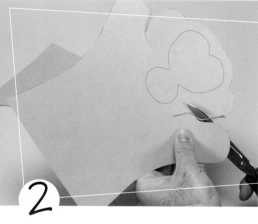

Trace the pattern on a piece of paper and cut it out. Use the paper to transfer the pattern to a piece of cardstock. The cardstock has a stronger edge and will last longer. Try to match a straight edge of the pattern with a straight edge in the cardstock. Cut out the cardstock pattern.

You may need to trim tight areas in the pattern multiple times so there's room for a marker or pencil tip to make an accurate mark.

Cutting fur

For cutting out fur using a pattern, lay the pattern on the back of the fabric, not on the fur itself. Trace lightly. Make sure the ink you use doesn't bleed through the fur.

Cut the fur using only the tips of your scissors. Try not to cut the shag of the fur as it will leave marks that are visible on your puppet.

Creating Eyes

I've spent a lifetime searching for the perfect puppet eyes. I started out sewing ice cream spoons to my puppet's face, but that didn't work well.

I've discovered many methods for creating eyes, including this one. Bubble stickers, made primarily for scrapbooking, look like big contact lenses. I created eye color patterns on my computer and stuck bubble circles over the eyes to give them a convex shape.

Basic Eyes

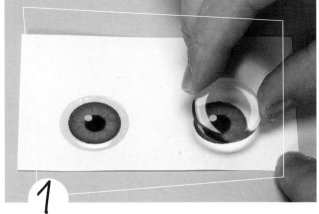

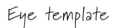

Make a color copy of the eyes from the template below. Enlarge or shrink the eyes as necessary to fit the puppet. Cover the eye with a plastic circle bubble sticker. Use larger stickers for larger eyes, and smaller stickers for smaller ones. The sticker should be slightly larger than the eye.

Cut out the eye and bubble sticker from the paper. Trim around the bubbles carefully using scissors. Place the eye on the surface of the puppet. Use adhesive to secure.

Professor Foaman's *travel tips*

Be careful when placing the bubble on the paper eyes. Line up the bubble slowly and then push it into place, pressing out any unwanted air bubbles.

Eye template

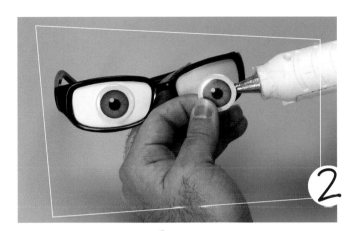
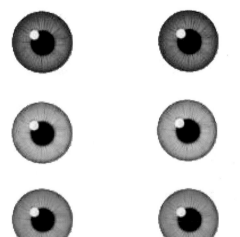

Working with foam

Foam is an excellent material for puppet making, and it's not hard to work with. This is one of my favorite secret techniques, and until now it was known to only a handful of people. With it, you can smooth and round the foam of a puppet, giving it a professional appearance.

This technique can potentially damage your puppet if done incorrectly. If there's an area that doesn't need to be smoothed because it's covered by hair or clothing, don't smooth it. Take time to practice before you work on a final project. You'll need a variable-speed, preferably at least five speed, Dremel in order to use the slower speeds for this technique. Wear a mask and safety goggles and keep the Dremel away from your face, loose clothing or hair as you work. Make sure there is no one near as you operate the Dremel.

Smoothing foam

1

2

For rounding corners, hold the puppet and the Dremel tightly and use light touches with the Dremel as you slowly move the puppet.

Find the center of a small circle of sandpaper. I use a 2¾" (7cm) diameter circle of medium, general purpose sandpaper, preferably 100 grit. Screw the sandpaper onto the screwhead bit of the Dremel. I've found that ⅛" (3mm) stainless steel mandrel bit works well. It comes with two washers that anchor the sandpaper. Hold the foam firmly and use only the lowest setting on the Dremel. Hold the Dremel firmly as well, keeping your finger on the on/off switch as you work. For smoothing flat areas, lightly brush the outside front edge of the sandpaper. Only work on the front edge of the sandpaper, not the sides or back, or you risk the Dremel ripping the foam.

3

For tight corners, press down the foam around the rough area so the foam you want to sand pops up. Sand carefully, keeping the area around the rough spots pressed down.

Basic Sewing

Verna Finly, a legendary ventriloquist puppet builder, taught me her method of sewing puppets, which she called the overhand basting stitch. With this method, you lace the edges of two fabric pieces with a needle and strong thread, drawing them together slowly and tightly to create an invisible seam.

There is a secret to fitting the fabric over a puppet. You need to make as few cuts on the fabric as possible and keep your cuts on each side of the puppet symmetical, then smooth it. Glue the back down first, keeping the face fabric tight and smoothing it where the fabric bunches, then pin the edges before sewing. Thanks, Verna!

Preparing the needle

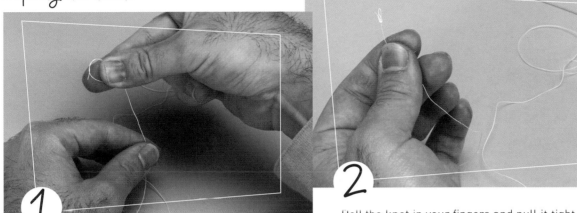

Thread the needle, and then tie the end of the thread in a big, loose knot.

Roll the knot in your fingers and pull it tight to keep the thread from sliding through the fabric.

Sewing Fabric

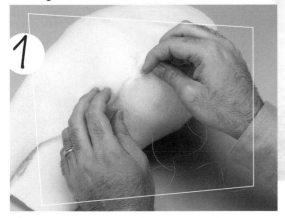

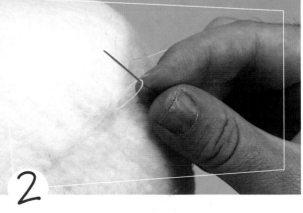

To sew two pieces of fabric together, push the needle through one piece of fabric near the seam, then back out. Move to the other piece of fabric and repeat. Make only five or six of these alternating, loose stitches that will look like the laces of a shoe. Tuck the edges of the fabric in and pull the stitches taut. Make adjustments to the fabric as needed with the tip of your needle.

Continue making alternating, loose stitches, tucking the fabric in and pulling the stitches taut every five or six stitches. To end a stitch and secure the thread, make several loops and pull them tight. Make one more loop and leave it loose. Bring the needle back through the loop and then pull it tight. This will knot the stitch closed. Trim the excess thread.

Meet the Citizens of Puppet Planet!

Puppet Planet is a place filled with creatures and characters you'll never forget, like the mysterious, mind-reading Parade Alien or the Sweatshirt Sheep who likes to sing off-key. You'll find a Strongman who wants nothing more than to make you strong, a rodent who became a big star on a string, and a monster who found its way out of my wife's closet. Honest!

These characters helped me become the puppeteer I am today. You'll discover techniques that will give your puppets a professional edge and a cool look. The puppets are the vehicles that will take you to new creative territories and help transport your audience's imagination during a show.

As you begin exploring Puppet Planet, you'll find the characters developing a personality and life of their own. The Field Guides will teach you how to perform with your creations. You'll discover how to use the strength of each design in your act. You'll also find insider's tips with secrets from a professional on performing, giving you the edge that will "WOW" the crowd. You'll find techniques such as using an invisible fishing line to pull a puppet or hiding your arm in a blanket to carry a character. The performance workshops give you ideas on how to set up the show for an audience. Pretty soon, you'll be a regular visitor to Puppet Planet.

Puppet Planet is fairly small right now (since the planet has just been discovered), but it's growing. You can play a big part in adding new citizens and share your creations with other puppeteers. Use the ideas in this book to create new characters, or come up with your own concepts. Send a picture of the new citizen to puppetk1t@yahoo.com, then find your character on my website at www.puppetkit.com. Spread the word about the book and the Puppet Planet project to your friends and family. Be a part of the underground puppet revolution and watch your character find a place online. Brainstorm new locales, new stories, new citizens and new characters. Let's see how huge we can make Puppet Planet!

So turn the page and start your journey through Puppet Planet. There's a whole new world waiting to be discovered.

Rod and Reel Rodent

You don't see many puppets performed with a fishing reel, but that's exactly what this mouse needed.

I was hired by the Indianapolis Symphony Orchestra to build all the puppets for their holiday show. During the performance, I was to pull a fishing line attached to a mouse hiding under the bed. On opening night, I got tangled up in the fishing line the first time I tried pulling the mouse. I couldn't move my hands and the mouse stopped dead in its tracks, so I just yanked. It was all I could do to keep the mouse moving. The mouse made a giant leap offstage. The antics of the mouse got a big laugh and we kept it in the show, but I wisely used a rod and reel after that first night so I didn't get caught up in my work again.

Tools and Materials

Small rod and reel fishing pole

Large plastic egg, 8" (20cm) long by 5" (13cm) wide

Short shag brown fur

Tan sheet foam

Three big black buttons

Needle and thread

Fishing line

Scissors

Pattern (page 72)

Cut the egg in half lengthwise using scissors. Place fur over one of the egg halves. Glue the fur on top first, then spread glue on the back of the egg. Flatten the fur over the back of the egg and pinch the sides to make hips. Pinch the excess fur in front of the egg to make a nose, then apply glue to the front of the egg.

Make sure the fur on the edge of the egg is firmly attached with glue, then trim the excess fur away from the bottom of the egg.

Fold the pinched fabric forward on the sides, where the rodent's hips would be. Glue the fold in place.

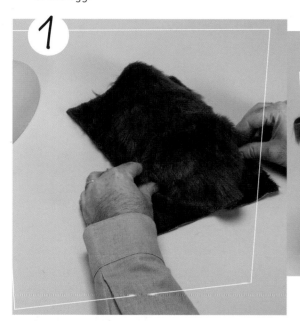

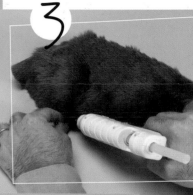

Professor Foaman's *travel tips*

Hot glue won't stick to some smooth surfaces. If you have trouble gluing the fur to the egg, use contact cement or another adhesive.

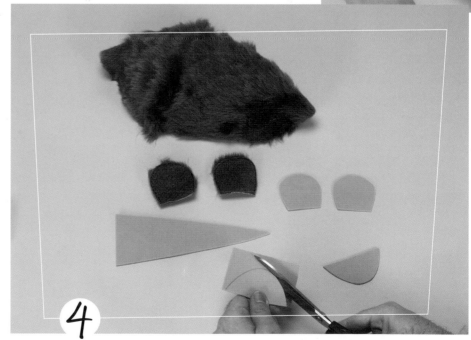

Using scissors and the pattern on page 72, cut out two rodent ears from tan sheet foam and two ears from the fur. Cut the tail and two rodent eyelids from tan sheet foam.

Professor Foaman's
travel tips

20

You could also sew the folds of the fur and foam tail, instead of gluing them.

Assemble the face. Glue a black button nose at the tip of the bunched fabric at the front of the egg. Glue the tan sheet foam ears inside the fur ears, then glue the ears on either side of the body in the middle of the egg. Glue the tan sheet foam eyes around the edges of the two remaining black buttons. Glue the eyes on either side of the face, between the ears and above the nose.

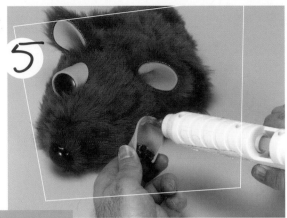

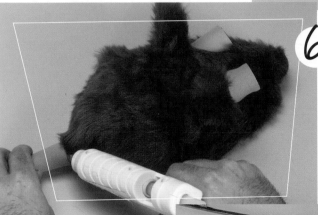

Fold the tail in half lengthwise and glue the edges together. Attach the tail to the back of the body.

Tie the fishing line from the rod and reel to the rodent, using a needle and thread to sew it to the front of the rodent below the nose.

Meet the Locals

I used the techniques in the Rod and Reel Rodent to make a creepy beetle using a juice bottle body, golf balls for eyes and some fur and straw for legs.

Meet the Locals

The egg makes a good basic shape for cute and furry creatures, such as a beaver.

Beaver

field guide to the Rod and Reel Rodent

This puppet works best as a surprise element in a show. Hide it first, then reveal it to the audience. Think about the timing of the rodent's movement. Is he running away or sneaking off? The intention of the movement is very important. Maybe he starts out slow, then stops, being proud of himself for being so sneaky, only to be startled by a noise and dart off stage. Let him do a little, cute laugh before being startled. With this puppet, it's all about timing.

Performance Workshop

If you want to be really clever with the path the rodent travels, you can arrange a system of removable pulleys that changes his direction. Imagine this rig as a connect-the-dots game with the rod and reel on one end, the rodent on the other, and each dot in between representing a pulley. As the rodent is reeled to a pulley, which could be as simple as fishing line and a hook, the string is detached, allowing the rodent to travel to the next pulley.

INSIDER tips

To keep other actors or puppeteers from getting caught up in the fishing line, you'll want to hold the end of the fishing pole against the floor as you reel in the line. This will keep the line from tripping the other performers.

Spoon Balloon Frog

Spoons have been an important part of my puppet-making career. Every time I go to the grocery store I find myself looking in the utensil aisle to see what new and interesting spoons might be available. Spoons make excellent eyes for a puppet. Ladles work great for this, but you can also use measuring spoons, soup spoons and regular tablespoons. All of these come in white plastic and can be painted or glued as needed.

With the Spoon Balloon Frog I decided to use the rounded shape of a ladle as the whole body of the frog and attach eyes to it. The handle became the perfect performance rod, so I didn't have to do a lot of major construction. It's a perfectly simple puppet with a balloon that adds an element of surprise.

Tools and Materials

Large plastic serving ladle

Green sheet foam

Small white balloon

3' (91cm) aquarium tubing

Two large circle bubble stickers

Dark and light green acrylic paint

Scissors

Paintbrush

Permanent ink marker

Electrical tape

Glue

Eye template (page 13)

Pattern (page 72)

Trace and cut out the body pattern on page 72 from green sheet foam. Glue the green foam body above the bowl-shaped part of the ladle. The legs will stick out from either side of the ladle. NOTE: You may need to adjust the pattern if your ladle is a different size.

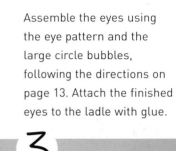

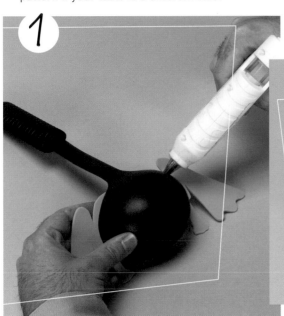

Paint the ladle using dark green acrylic paint. Leave space for the eyes on the spoon. Paint the green sheet foam feet of the frog using dark green acrylic paint, leaving an unpainted border on the feet.

Assemble the eyes using the eye pattern and the large circle bubbles, following the directions on page 13. Attach the finished eyes to the ladle with glue.

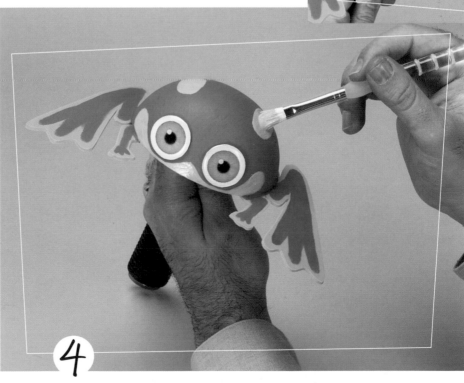

Professor Foaman's *travel tips*

Contact cement will secure foam to the spoon better than hot glue.

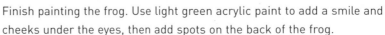

Finish painting the frog. Use light green acrylic paint to add a smile and cheeks under the eyes, then add spots on the back of the frog.

Professor Foaman's
travel tips

If you use a larger balloon, you may need to cut a larger mouth opening in the sheet foam.

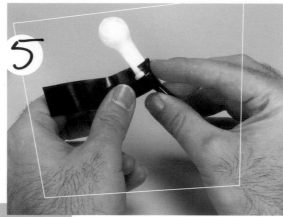

5 Place the balloon over one end of the aquarium tubing, then use electrical tape to hold the balloon in place. Make sure the tape secures the balloon and no air escapes between the balloon and the tubing.

6 Run the end of the tubing without the balloon through the mouth of the frog, through the body and down the handle of the ladle until the balloon is hidden inside the mouth of the frog. Tape the tubing to the handle, just below the frog. Run the end of the tubing without the balloon through the hook on the bottom of the ladle. NOTE: If there is no hook, just tape the tubing in place at the end of the ladle.

7 Add a nose and a smile to the frog's face with a permanent ink marker.

Meet the Locals

The thing I like most about this puppet is that you can be as colorful and creative as you want to be. Sure, most frogs are green, but what about all of the exotic, unknown frogs of the rainforest? You can just imagine the colorful frogs and lizards that haven't yet been discovered.

field guide to the Spoon Balloon Frog

Sometimes the simplest puppets are the best. This statement is especially true of the Spoon Balloon Frog. You get a lot of control and animation with this small puppet. When you take a simple approach to a performance and then add a cool gimmick, like the balloon, you get a big reaction from the audience. Hold back your funny gimmick for the right moment for an even bigger laugh. Comic timing is the name of the game, and this puppet has the potential to knock them dead. Try to find music or a script that builds up the anticipation to that perfect moment.

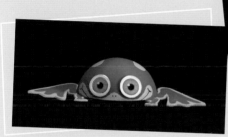

Jumping
Time your movement and the audience will believe the frog is jumping.

Taking a breath
Hold the surprise of seeing the frog breathe for the right moment to add to the audience's reaction.

Resting
Placing the frog against a black background helps hide the spoon.

Performance Workshop

You could build a box and pretend you are keeping the frog as a pet. Cut out the back of the box so you have room to perform in the frog's "cage." Any tabletop works well as a quick stage for the Spoon Balloon Frog.

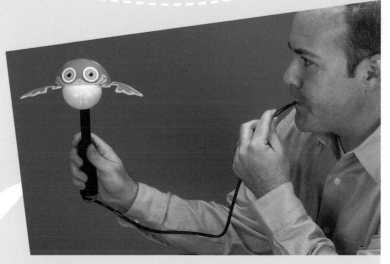

INSIDER tips

Using the Spoon Balloon Frog is simple. Just hold the handle in one hand while you blow into the other end of the tubing. Make sure you hold the frog loosely, so the balloon has room to expand.

Shoe Box Monster

I'm always looking for new puppet-making materials, so I'm constantly asking myself questions when I enter a store. Can I make eyes out of this or can I use that to make a nose? Is that the right measuring spoon to create eyes for my new puppet, or will that plastic orange work as a nose? Most of the time I let the materials dictate the final character design. In this way, a shopping trip becomes a creative journey.

After watching me shop for puppet supplies, my wife told me she will never look at some of the stores I go to in the same way. In this project, however, I didn't have to leave the house. My wife is the proud owner of over two hundred pairs of shoes. In her closet were enough styles and shapes of shoe boxes for me to make the Shoe Box Puppet.

Tools and Materials

Shoe box	White sheet foam	Permanent ink marker
1" (3cm) soft foam rubber	Two large white pom-poms	Ruler
Long shag dark brown fur	Two small black pom-poms	Clear tape
Red and pink construction paper	Scissors	Glue

Remove the lid of the shoe box. Find the middle of both long sides of the lower half of the shoe box. Cut the box on these middle lines, leaving the bottom of the box uncut.

Fold the lower box in half. Cut two pieces of soft foam rubber to fit inside the folded box halves. Cut a notch for your thumb in one piece of foam, placing the notch against the center fold. Glue the foam inside the box. Glue only the outer edges of the unnotched foam, leaving room for your fingers to slide beneath the foam when you manipulate the mouth.

Cut a short side off the lid of the box. Tape it above the unnotched foam, leaving room for your fingers to slide under the foam. Trim the edges of the box so all four sides are even. This will be the top of your Shoe Box Monster.

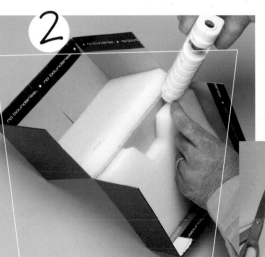

Professor Foaman's
travel tips

Decorate the brain of your Shoe Box Monster with crazy paper, such as gift wrapping paper.

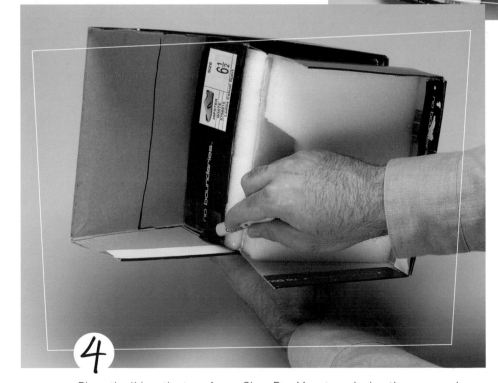

Place the lid on the top of your Shoe Box Monster, placing the open end in the back. Trace the back side of the lid against the back of the Shoe Box Monster top, creating a flap long enough to fold over the back. Draw lines across the sides of the lid, marking an area that is the same width as the sides of the box. Cut the lid on the lines.

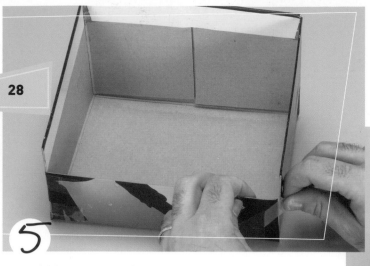

Place the lid on the Shoe Box Monster top. Position the white pom-poms on the lid, using the fold as the mouth. Trace around the pom-pom eyes, then put them aside and remove the lid. Cut out the area you traced from the lid.

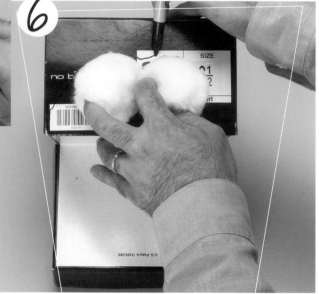

5 Make a new, smaller lid by folding the flap down and taping it to the existing sides of the lid. Check that the lid fits the top of the Shoe Box Monster. Make adjustments as necessary.

7 Assemble the face. Place the lid back on the box and glue the eyes where you positioned them earlier. The lid should fit over the eyes. Glue small black pom-pom pupils to the eyes. Cut a piece of red construction paper for the mouth and glue it in place, trimming as necessary. Make sure to fold the mouth closed before gluing the paper, so it doesn't wrinkle when the mouth closes. Add pink construction paper gums, then freehand cut jagged teeth from white sheet foam and glue them over the pink gums.

8 For the monster brain, glue pink construction paper to the sides, not the lid, of the Shoe Box Monster top. Trim the pink construction paper around the eyes. Scribble lines in the brain for brain wrinkles.

9 Use glue to cover the lid and the lower sides of the box with fur. Trim the fur as necessary.

Meet the Locals

Think of other creatures and shapes you can make with a shoe box, then use the basic design and your imagination to make it unique. This shoe box reminded me of a hungry mailbox. A cardboard flag, a big mouth in the front, eyes made out of unpainted styrofoam pears and a dyed foam tongue was all it needed.

field guide to the Shoe Box Monster

One way to incorporate your monster into a show is to make the monster hold something important to your scene. You could hold a raffle with names on pieces of paper in the Shoe Box Monster's head. Have another character pick a winner. Or, attach a rod to one piece of paper and have the Monster blow it out of his head. When the Monster takes a deep breath, pop the name out and have it float down and into another character's hand.

What's on the monster's mind?

"Shew! Have I got a lotta stuff tah do! I better write it all down. First I got to drive my pet bird, Chirpy-kins, to the vet for a check-up, then I have to pick up an anniversary card for my sweetie and get it all done before the baseball game this afternoon. I hope it doesn't rain!"

INSIDER tips

Hold the Shoe Box Monster by placing your fingers under the foam and manipulating the puppet with your thumb in the notch. You may want to glue a strip of felt or rubber on the cardboard to give your thumb and fingers a better grip.

Pillow Buddy

I've been involved in a lot of puppet shows with characters that are inanimate objects that "come to life." When I build a puppet like this, I try to keep the original shape of the object while giving it a personality. This can be difficult to do when you want to make a puppet that is flexible. If the object is made of plastic or metal, it can be hard to manipulate.

Fortunately, pillows aren't made of plastic or metal. They are the perfect inanimate object to come to life. The Pillow Buddy is a lightweight and flexible puppet that can still be used for its original purpose, making it a great personal sidekick for younger puppeteers or a good place to take a nap.

Tools and Materials

Pillow (a 16" [41cm] square couch pillow was used for this puppet)

Black sheet foam

Short shag off-white fur

Long shag dark brown fur

Clasp eyes (30mm)

Needle and thread (white or off-white thread was used for this puppet)

Scissors

Glue

Pattern (page 72)

Cut a piece of off-white, short shag fur that is as wide as the pillow but twice as tall. Line up the sides and bottom of the fur with the sides and bottom of the pillow, then sew the edges of the fur around the left, right and bottom edges of the pillow, with the excess fur hanging over the top.

Fold the fur against the top edge of the pillow, letting the excess hang over the front. Sew the inside edge of the fur against the top edge of the pillow.

Fold the excess fur into two equal folds over the top of the pillow, leaving enough extra fur to cover the folded edges in the back. Pinch the folds together on both sides of the pillow.

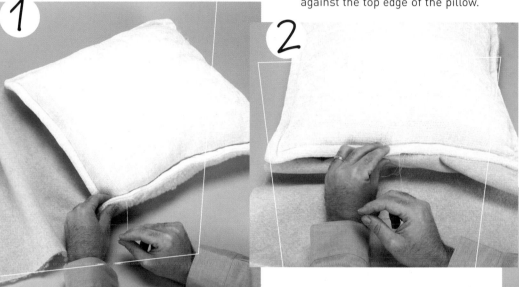

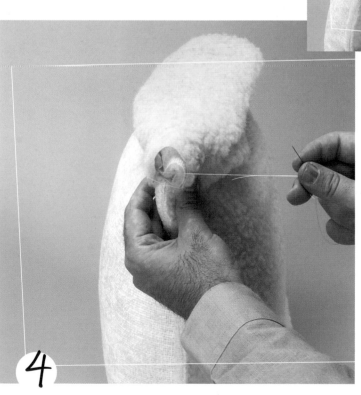

Sew the pinched folds together on either side of the pillow. Sew through all the layers of fur, securing the folds to the top of the pillow.

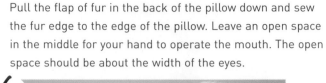

5

Pull the flap of fur in the back of the pillow down and sew the fur edge to the edge of the pillow. Leave an open space in the middle for your hand to operate the mouth. The open space should be about the width of the eyes.

Assemble the eyes. Using the pattern on page 72, cut out the eyelashes from black sheet foam, turning the pattern over for the second eye. Place the eyelashes behind the eyes, trimming the eyelashes for smaller eyes. Position the eyes on the top fold of fur, keeping the eyes about 2½" (6cm) apart, then use scissors to make a slit in the top of the folded fur beneath the eyes. Attach the eyes using the clasp.

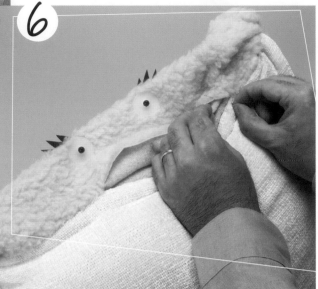

6

7

Take a scrap of dark, long shag fur and glue it behind the eyes, covering the clasps and letting the strands of fur peek over the head for hair. Next, cut out the mouth from black sheet foam using the pattern on page 72 and glue it inside the mouth. Make sure the foam is folded in the middle and it will open as the mouth opens.

8

Make a single stitch through all three layers of fur on either side of the mouth. This will keep the face from flopping backward and create a chin for the puppet.

Meet the Locals

Pillows come in a lot of shapes and sizes. Look for fur that matches the creature you want to create, and then sew the face together. Roll up more fur to add ears or paws. I'm not sure what kind of creature this is, but he looks like he might lick you in the face.

field guide to the Pillow Buddy

Pillow Buddy's soft, movable face is great for creating expressions. By simply bending your fingers around, you can build up a library of expressions that are perfect for reactions to events onstage. You could have Pillow Buddy be surprised at how happy the audience is feeling, give a kiss to the person with the biggest smile, compare grumpy faces, and then talk about the differences between happy and angry.

Happy
An open mouth will make Pillow Buddy look happy.

Grumpy
Curl the bottom lip over the top for a grumpy look.

Kissing
This is tricky. Arch your fingers in an "O" shape, then pinch them together to blow a kiss to the crowd. Practice to get the expression perfect.

INSIDER tips

Pillow Buddy's design allows for one of your hands to be free to hold a book. You can read and have Pillow Buddy make comments about the story. Pillow Buddy is a lot like a ventriloquist figure in the way you perform, because you can tuck the puppet close to your body and no one can see your arm. You have to believe Pillow Buddy is real, or you'll lose the audience. Once you've convinced an audience that Pillow Buddy is real, the show will come alive.

Crafty Cockatoo

I love to lead puppet workshops. In every workshop there is a point where people aren't looking for directions and creativity conquers fear. People feel an inspirational surge as the vision of a puppet suddenly takes over. Up to this moment I get a lot of questions and blank stares as I discuss the puppets, but when this transformation occurs there's no stopping the new characters that pop into the imagination and demand to be made.

I designed the Crafty Cockatoo with this process in mind. There are only a few steps you need to complete before you can dive right into crafting the character that has come to life in your imagination. Go out on a limb and be as crafty and crazy as you want.

Tools and Materials

Two plastic milk jugs	Blue feathers	Needle and thread
Hair clip	Pink feather boa	Four cable ties
Two blue baby booties	Clasp eyes	Permanent ink marker
Stuffing	Scissors (heavy scissors work best for this project)	Ruler
Orange sheet foam		Glue
Red felt	Standard hole punch	Pattern (page 73)

Cut the nozzle from a milk jug. Place the hair clip over the hole. Mark where cable ties will attach the clip to the jug. Use scissors or a large hole punch to punch holes through the marks. Using the holes and the cable ties, lash the hair clip to the top of the milk jug. Make sure you lash only the bottom half of the clip. Trim the cable ties.

Following the patterns on page 73, trace and cut out the beak and feet patterns from the orange sheet foam and the tongue from red felt. Place the bottom beak around the hair clip. Trace the inside edge of the pattern on the milk jug, drawing a line $\frac{1}{4}$" (6mm) in front of the hair clip and ignoring the tabs on either side of the pattern. Remove the beak and cut out the bowl-shaped area you just traced in front of the hair clip.

Glue the feet to the bottom front of the milk jug. Glue down the back of the bottom beak, then glue the two tabs inside the milk jug, securing the bottom beak in place. Glue the tongue to the lower beak, wrapping the square end of the tongue under the beak.

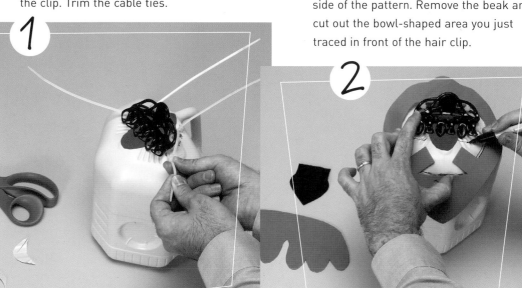

1

2

3

Professor Foaman's *travel tips*

Make "rivets" of hot glue to secure the foam to the jug. Punch a hole in the milk jug where the foam is attached, then fill the hole with a large dot of glue. This will help secure the foam. Contact cement will also work.

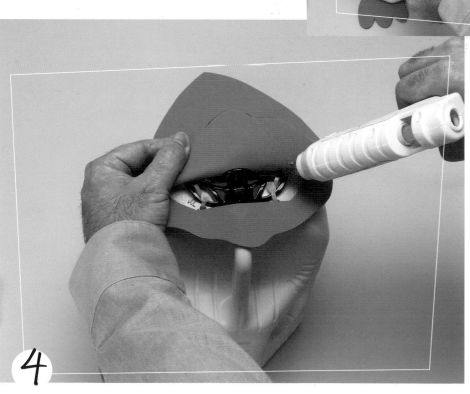

4

Glue the upper beak to the upper half of the hair clip. Do not glue the beak to the grip on the hair clip, only the clip itself. Make sure you leave room beneath the foam for your fingers to manipulate the clip and move the beak.

Professor Foaman's
travel tips

You might have to make the holes bigger in the milk jug. When necessary, twist a blade of the scissors in the hole to widen it.

36

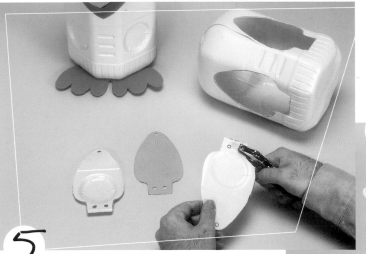

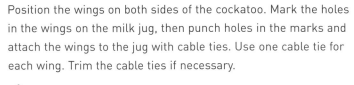

Position the wings on both sides of the cockatoo. Mark the holes in the wings on the milk jug, then punch holes in the marks and attach the wings to the jug with cable ties. Use one cable tie for each wing. Trim the cable ties if necessary.

6

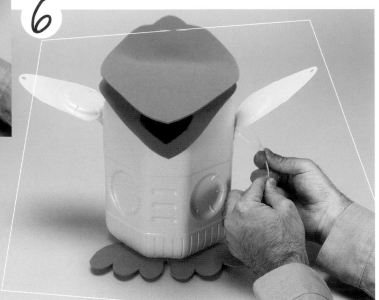

5

Use the wing pattern on page 73 to cut out two wings from the second milk jug. Use a hole punch to make the holes in the wings where indicated on the pattern.

7

Trim the elastic band from the baby booties. Use stuffing to fill the booties, then place an eye on each of the booties. When you are satisfied with the position of the eyes, clasp the eyes in place and sew the back of the booties closed.

8

Glue the eyes together, then glue both eyes to the top of the beak in front of the hair clip, helping to hide the clip. Glue the boa and blue feathers around the back of the beak and eyes. Glue blue feathers on the wings. Continue decorating the Crafty Cockatoo until you are satisfied with the results. You may add feathers to the front of the milk jug or under the wings if you like.

9

Tie a 3' (91cm) long thread from the hole at the end of one wing to the hole at the end of the other wing. Trim if necessary.

Meet the Locals

I used a green laundry detergent bottle and foam to create an alligator, and a white laundry detergent bottle, a banana clip and some black fur to create a penguin. What kind of creatures do you have hiding in your cupboard?

field guide to the Crafty Cockatoo

With a little ingenuity, the Crafty Cockatoo can be a useful tool during performances. Why not cut a big hole for the mouth and make a game of Cockatoo Catch? Turn the bird's beak into a Crafty Coin Catcher and get rid of your old piggy bank, or make a Crafty Cockatoo tissue dispenser and cure your sick friends with laughter.

Performance Workshop

The Crafty Cockatoo can be a great addition to a show. With his big eyes and colorful feathers, the Cockatoo can be a crazy character. Sit him on someone's shoulder while you hide behind them and perform the Cockatoo. Give him a funny voice, with loud squawks and high-pitched whistles, and let him make sarcastic comments throughout the show.

INSIDER tips

Even though the Crafty Cockatoo is meant to be more of a hand puppet, you can also add more strings to do some simple marionette-type movements. In addition to wings, you could add big eyebrows, a tail, floppy legs or an expressive topknot. Just make a felt or plastic body part, tie a length of string to it, and pull it from above or below. You may have to attach a spring so the body part can pop back into place.

Mechanical Stagehand

Once, when my best friend Ed and I needed just one more act for the show, we used a furry glove as a puppet. It popped up from the stage so it seemed like it was a big creature hiding just below. That way we didn't have to make the whole puppet, just the glove. We let the audience imagine what the rest of the lurking creature looked like. We could use it to move props, show a sign, or pull a character offstage.

Since then, I've experimented with the concept and came up with a new twist by adding a mechanical element. I found that I could get a little more reach on stage by extending the hand out on a salad tong. The thumb still works to pick up or hold things. Now I could even pass a rubber chicken across the stage with no problem. Now that's comedy!

Tools and Materials

Plastic sign	Pink felt	Cable ties
Serving tongs	Needle and thread	Permanent ink pen
Long shag dark brown fur	Scissors	Glue
Short shag orange fur	Drill and bit	Pattern (page 73)

Using the pattern on page 73, cut out the fingers and thumb from the thick plastic of a sign. Drill holes in the plastic, following the markings on the pattern.

Use cable ties and the holes you just made to attach the plastic fingers and thumb to the serving tong. Attach the fingers on one side of the tong and the thumb to the other. Trim the cable ties.

Fold a piece of short shag fur across the inside of the hand. With the fur folded in the middle, trace around the thumb and fingers, leaving a small border around the plastic. Cut along the lines you traced, leaving the folded fur in the middle uncut. Place this fur piece back over the inside of the hands, gluing it in place. Make large "rivets" of glue inside the drilled holes of the thumb and fingers to hold the fur in place. See page 35 for more information on making rivets of glue.

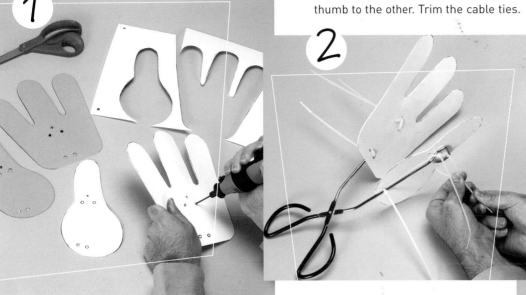

1

2

3

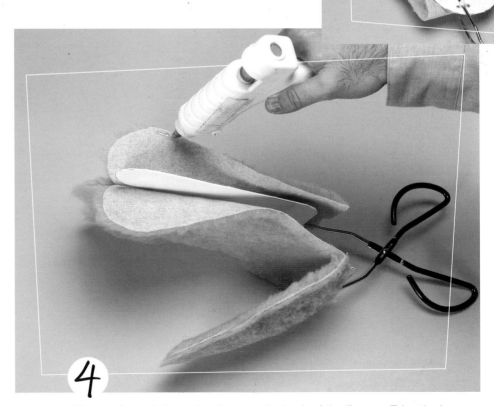

Professor Foaman's *travel tips*

You can use any type of thick, rigid plastic to make the thumb and hand of the Mechanical Stagehand. A plastic sign is fairly easy to find, but large milk jugs, a plastic storage tub or plastic food containers will also work.

4

Place a piece of short shag fur over the back of the fingers. Trim the fur following the edge of the fingers, leaving a small border around the plastic. Cut between the fingers, then trim the fur 1" (3cm) below the bottom of the plastic fingers. Glue the fur around the plastic, following the edge of the fingers. Do the same for the thumb side of the hand.

Professor Foaman's
travel tips

Rather than glue the sleeve around the hand, you may want to sew it in place. This will hold the fur more securely.

40

Freehand cut fingernails out of pink felt for the Stagehand, and glue them on the outside of the fingers and thumb. Add a few long shag fur spots to the back of the hand.

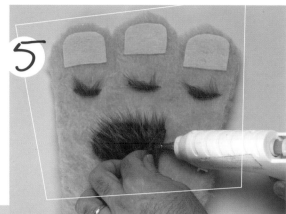

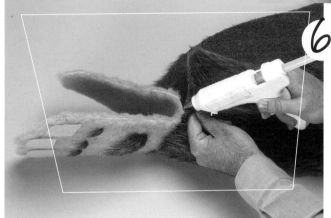

Create a sleeve for the hand. Lay the hand on a large piece of long shag fur. Roll it over the base of the hand. Cut the near end so it fits over the opened tongs, but widens out so you can operate the hand and use the tongs easily. Glue the serving tongs to the fur at the base of the hand, then glue the fur closed so the tongs are inside the sleeve.

Meet the Locals

Who said the Stagehand had to be a brute? Add a costume to the Stagehand and he can be a gentleman, ready to sweep a lady off her feet with one hand and show her a night on the town!

field guide to the Mechanical Stagehand

Because you have extra reach with the Mechanical Stagehand, you can maneuver it through some tricky staging areas like a barrel, window or door. Think of ways to get the full mechanical use out of your Mechanical Stagehand. Your story could call for a giant to pick up a golden egg, a big monkey to carry off a beautiful lady, or a large pinching crab to cut a fishing line and save our halibut hero from the evil fisherman.

You'll have to build or find props that are easy for the Mechanical Stagehand to hold. The weight and placement of these props are crucial in doing a well-timed performance. Make sure the hand can easily pick up and carry the props in your show.

Hello? Oh, it's for you.

The Mechanical Stagehand is great for handing props to other characters or the audience. You can get a good extension and pass something a long way. Try passing a letter from a mailbox or a handkerchief to a maiden in distress.

Welcome to Puppet Planet!

A sign can be a great comic ploy. It can warn the hero in your play or instruct the audience to applaud or turn off their cell phones. Whatever the message, it will be a funny surprise.

And now for the Puppet Planet revue. . . AAAH!!

Sometimes you have to get tough with an out-of-control Sweatshirt Sheep. When he doesn't want to stop singing, you can use the Mechanical Stagehand to escort him quickly offstage.

INSIDER tips

To get the maximum reach out of your Mechanical Stagehand, make the sleeve as long as your arm so you can really get it out there without anyone seeing your clothing. Always make more length than you need so there won't be any embarrassing moments such as having the giant in Jack and the Beanstalk suddenly wearing the Hawaiian shirt everyone saw you wearing before the show.

Dress up your Mechanical Stagehand to fit the occasion. Why not give him a striped shirt and handcuffs when he gets arrested for getting "out of hand" at a workers' strike?

Sweatshirt Sheep

One of the things I would do as a kid when I didn't have a puppet to perform was pull my arm inside the sleeve of a sweatshirt and push the elastic wristband into my hand to make a quick puppet. I could entertain at any time.

This puppet adds to that simple idea to make a really cute sheep. You'll need to cut up your sweatshirt, so don't use a favorite, but once you start, you may find this puppet is so fun you'll be inspired to make a whole flock of sheep. You might even have to take a nap after counting them all.

Tools and Materials

Sweatshirt	Red felt	Permanent ink marker
Plastic food container lid (about 4" [10cm] in diameter and should fit in the sleeve)	Long shag gray fur	Scissors
	Two puppet eyes (special effect eyes or pom-poms will also work)	Glue
Stuffing		Pattern (page 72)

Cut the sleeve from a sweatshirt. Set the sleeve aside. Using the pattern on page 72, cut two ears and two legs from the leftover sweatshirt fabric. Cut through only one layer of the fabric.

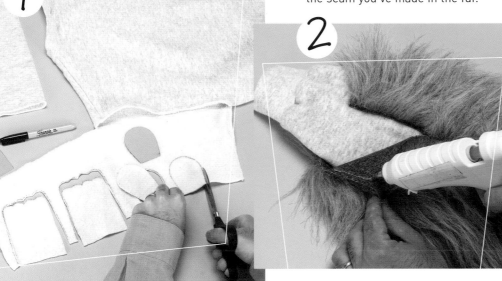

Wrap the fur around the sleeve of the sweatshirt, leaving the cuff and the top 2" (5cm) of the sleeve free of fur. Trim the fur to fit the sleeve. Glue the fur around the sleeve, going from the bottom to the top and gluing the seam of the fur closed against the sleeve. Do not glue the top of the fur on the side opposite the seam you've made in the fur.

Cut a piece of red felt using the food container lid as a pattern. Glue the felt on the top of the lid. This will be the mouth of the Sweat-shirt Sheep.

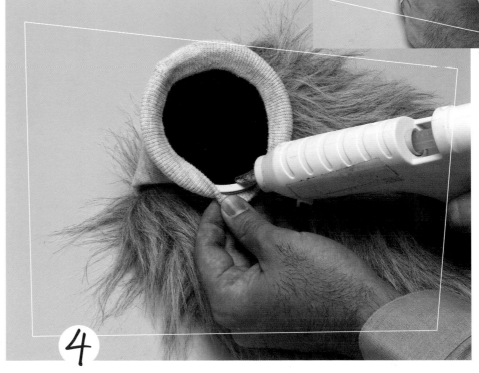

Using the pattern on page 72

Professor Foaman's *travel tips*

Try to find a plastic food container lid that fits perfectly inside the wrist opening of your sweatshirt. If you need a little more grip on the inside of the puppet mouth for your fingers, glue felt to the underside of the lid.

Place the mouth inside the sleeve of the sweatshirt with the red facing out. Make sure there is an even lip of sweatshirt fabric around the mouth, then glue the fabric around the edge of the mouth, covering the plastic lip of the lid.

Professor Foaman's
travel tips

If you work carefully, you should have enough fabric in one sweatshirt for two sweatshirt sheep, using one whole sleeve for each sheep.

44

Plan the position of the eyes on the top of the head at the edge of the fur. Working with one eye at a time, wrap the fur around the back of the eye and glue the fur and eye in place. Fold the ears in half and glue the bottom closed, then attach an ear beside each eye on either side of the face.

Roll the legs and glue the edges together, leaving one end open. Fill the legs with stuffing, then glue each leg closed. Attach the legs on either side of the puppet, about 3" (8cm) from the top of the fur. Spread the long shag fur apart and glue the leg against the fabric beneath the fur. Pinch the material at the edge of the mouth forward, then glue it just behind the mouth.

Meet the Locals

This is the Sweatshirt Sheep's nemesis, the Sweatshirt Lion. This big, dumb lion chases our hero, but he can't outwit the clever sheep! Don't worry; this Lion is a big softy, with pom-pom eyes and a fuzzy mane.

field guide to the Sweatshirt Sheep

Not only is the Sweatshirt Sheep easy to make, but he's easy to perform. The plastic lid is very flexible and should help create some extreme expressions. String the expressions together with a small cast of sheep and you could do a Sweatshirt Sheep Soap Opera.

Dizzy

Twisting your fingers like you're turning a doorknob will make the sheep appear dizzy. Have him stagger and knock over a few set pieces.

Surprise

If your sheep suddenly goes from closed-mouthed to wide-mouthed, he will look surprised. He may even remain motionless for several minutes. What will your other characters do?

Embarrassed

Curl your fingers into a fist to make the Sweatshirt Sheep look embarrassed. Have him slowly crawl behind a piece of furniture, or run away.

Excited

Holding the sheep's mouth partially open while bobbing his head up and down will make the sheep look excited. He could hop up and down and run around the stage, chew on the furniture and bounce on the sofa until the other characters have to tie him down or he passes out from exhaustion.

INSIDER tips

A blanket wrapped around the sheep will cover up your arm as you do a ventriloquist-style performance. Signal nap time to kids by singing a lullaby with your sheep. If the Sweatshirt Sheep forgets the song and makes up silly words, you may have to threaten no sheep snacks until he sings it the right way. Reacting and bantering with the Sweatshirt Sheep will be entertaining and make for a more realistic show.

Monkey Mitten

My first introduction into television puppetry was on a local Indianapolis TV show called "Time For Timothy." To me, the characters were just as famous as anyone else on TV. The puppets were very simple, but I remember they had great expressions. I convinced the producers to let me make puppets for the show, and I found you could make great characters that were easy to perform using latex. The result was a success, and I got the feel for working on television in a three-camera style shoot, something I got to do a lot of when I was hired to work on Sesame Street.

Monkey Mitten uses the same process as those puppets from "Time For Timothy." It's a simple puppet, but the latex gives him a lot of facial expressions and detail. With a mouth like this, he can "ook" and "eek" and eat bananas all day long.

Tools and Materials

Polymer clay (Super Sculpey)

Plaster (Ultracal 30)

Latex rubber

Short shag orange fur

Clasp eyes

Tan and black acrylic paint

Plastic wrap

Pencil

Paintbrush

Container

Baby powder (optional)

Two paper plates

Scissors

Needle and thread (optional)

Glue

Pattern (page 74)

Roll balls of clay and assemble them on paper plates to make a face and two hands. Roll a large ball for the middle of the face, a smaller ball for the chin, and four small balls for the ears and eyes. Roll a small ball for each palm and smaller balls for the fingers. Add extra clay to the thumbs. Begin molding the balls of clay to form the face and hands. Flatten the balls for the ears, eyes and fingers.

Continue molding until you're satisfied with the basic shape. Add fine details, such as wrinkles and eyelashes, by laying plastic wrap over the clay and drawing lines with a pencil or your fingernail. Finish by checking the mold against the Monkey Mitten pattern on page 74. The face should be about 5" (13cm) wide, including ears, and 3" (8cm) long. The hands are 2½" (6cm) long and 2" (5cm) wide. Make adjustments to the face and hands as necessary to fit the pattern.

Mix up plaster, following the directions on the package. When finished, brush the plaster carefully over the clay face and hands, making sure the plaster fills all the small details in the clay.

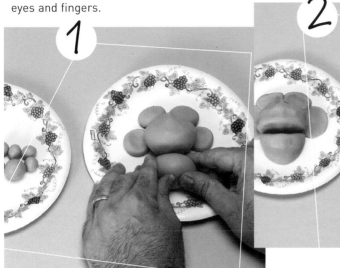

Pour a thick layer of plaster over the clay, keeping just enough of a lip to make sure the plaster doesn't spread beyond the plates. When dry, pry the clay out of the dried plaster.

Mix tan acrylic paint to add color to the latex. Add the acrylic paint slowly until you're satisfied with the color. NOTE: The latex dries a shade darker than it appears while wet. Remember this as you mix the acrylic paint in the latex.

When the latex is dry, peel it out of the mold. Trim the edges of the latex face and hands, leaving a small border of latex on the outside edge of the face to help secure it to the fur.

6

Brush a thin first layer of latex in the plaster molds. Be sloppy, covering the inside of the mold and over the edges. Let the latex dry for an hour, then add another layer following the same directions. Continue until you've made four thin layers to complete the latex face and hands.

7

8

Trace and cut out the monkey pattern found on page 74 from the fur. For the front of the monkey, cut out the face. Do not trace or cut out the face from the back of the monkey.

Professor Foaman's travel tips

There are times the latex will stick to itself. You may want to sprinkle some baby powder on the latex before you peel it out of the mold.

9

Glue the latex face to the front of the monkey. Glue the ears to the fur, then glue the edge of the face inside the fur. When the glue is dry, clip a small hole in the latex of the eyes, then add the clasp eyes to the monkey.

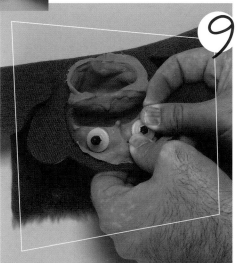

10

Sew or glue the edges of the front and back of the body together, making sure not to glue the bottom of the monkey. Leave space for your hands to fit inside the monkey. Glue the hands on the puppet. Paint the inside of the mouth with black acrylic paint, adding a bit of latex to the paint. Use the black paint as sparingly as possible.

Meet the Locals

Use the basic shape of this puppet to create a whole scene of characters. The clay makes it easy to create features for the puppet, and the latex makes it fun to contort the face into extreme expressions. Come up with a story for your characters. This poor cat crossed the wrong bridge and woke up a troll. A chase scene across the stage is always fun for the audience.

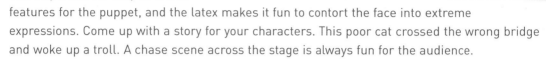

field guide to the Monkey Mitten

When performing the Monkey Mitten, don't be afraid to go crazy. Monkeys can be wild and unpredictable and that gives you license to play around more than you normally would. Most times you want your puppet to be subtle, so you can show a wide range of emotions. The Monkey Mitten has manic energy that's always cute. Let the other characters do Shakespeare, while you release your inner monkey!

Happy

The monkey is the perfect comic relief mechanism in a play. Have him pop in during a lull in the action, especially if it breaks up a tense moment. This will get a laugh because the audience wants to break the tension.

Shocked

Something really big has to happen to surprise a monkey. Play up the shock value of your monkey's discovery.

Bashful

Sometimes the monkey can be scary to children. If the monkey appears bashful, the child may try to soothe the monkey. Once you've regained the child's trust, let the monkey go back to his antics.

Parade Alien

For years I've used an opaque projector to enlarge small patterns and make larger-than-life puppets. I usually start with a small version of my character. The little pattern is then projected like a movie to be traced, cut out and glued together. The result is a big version of the small puppet I started with.

The Parade Alien could be a big puppet that's easy to perform. Enlarge this pattern and follow the steps to stitch it together. Use a light stuffing material, then find a few people to hold the poles and join a parade. But, you don't have to make a giant puppet that walks down the street or takes over the auditorium stage. This pattern also makes a smaller puppet that is perfect for parading around your home or classroom.

Tools and Materials

Orange, black and light blue felt	Two large circle bubble stickers	Needle and thread
One ½" (12mm) dowel rod	Black acrylic paint	Scissors
Two ¼" (6mm) dowel rods	Paintbrush	Small plate or palette
Stuffing	Pen or pencil	Glue
27" (69cm) of rope	Sewing machine	Eye template (page 13)
		Pattern (page 74)

Cut out the patterns on page 74 from the orange and light blue felt. You should have two orange arms and one orange body, two blue head pieces, four blue hand pieces and four blue feet pieces, and two blue ear pieces.

Sew the two head pieces together using a sewing machine and thread. Sew two of the felt hand pieces together, using stitching to shape the fingers, to create a hand. Repeat for the second hand. Do the same for the feet, using stitching to create toes. Roll the arms and body pieces and sew them closed. Leave the ends open, hemming the edges.

Pull all the fabric pieces right side out to hide the seams. You should have a head, two feet, two hands, two arms and a body. Fill the head with stuffing, then sew the neck shut with a needle and thread.

Paint the dowel rods black using acrylic paint and a paintbrush. Let dry before continuing.

Tie the 27" (69cm) rope around the top of the larger dowel rod, making sure both ends of the rope are the same length. Cut a small slit 2" (5cm) up from the chin in the back of the alien's head. Insert 5" (13cm) of the larger dowel rod through the slit and into the stuffed head, leaving the rope just outside the alien's head.

Slide the sleeves up the ends of the 27" (69cm) rope to the base of the head. Make a small slit 2" (5cm) from the end of both sleeves and insert a smaller dowel into the slit. For both arms, tie the rope to the dowel. Put the end of the dowel into the thumb of the hand, and the end of the rope into a finger. If you like, glue the cuff of the sleeve to the hand.

Slide the body piece up the large dowel to the neck and glue it in place just beneath the head, hiding the ropes. Glue the feet in place at the bottom front of the body.

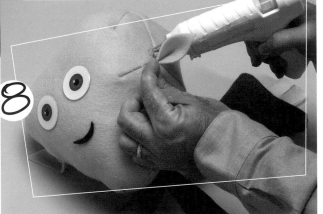

Assemble the face. Freehand draw a mouth on a piece of black felt. Cut it out and glue it on the face. Make two eyes, following the directions on page 13, and glue them to the face. Fold and glue the bottom of the ears closed, then glue the ears to either side of the head.

Meet the Locals

Even Puppet Planet needs a Santa! A few variations to the Parade Alien created this Santa. Add a beard and boots, for example, and make the body a little larger on the bottom. To make the face wider on the bottom, turn the head upside down. A cap hides the top of his jolly head.

field guide to the Parade Alien

The Parade Alien is meant to be performed with the puppeteer(s) in plain view. For a very large Parade Alien you could have a person working each arm, one person working the body and head, and another person operating a prop that the puppet could carry. The actions need to be choreographed and practiced as a team to make a believable character.

With practice, one puppeteer can work all of the rods so you want to keep the Parade Alien small and you can include as many puppets as possible in a scene. Either way the Parade Puppet is meant to be a special effect or an iconic figure. He doesn't need to make a lot of movements or expressions to be appreciated. He just needs to show up and do a few strong gestures to get a big reaction from a crowd.

I come in peace

Use this gesture at the beginning of a performance. It shows that the alien means no harm and wants to be friends. Try to have the alien make eye contact with people and it will be more meaningful.

Welcome

Use this pose no matter what is happening, and it will look as if your alien is "all knowing" and wise. It works well if it's accompanied by a wave or blowing a kiss.

Peekaboo

To warm up a crowd you can add a bit of playfulness with a game of peekaboo. It's easier if you have a person working each arm, but it can be done with one puppeteer. Try other gestures, such as high fives, handshakes and hugs to loosen up the crowd.

I can read your thoughts . . .

If you come upon a stubborn onlooker, you can make light of the situation by reading his thoughts. Put one of the alien's hands on the person's head and the other on the alien's head. It won't always get a laugh, but at least it shows you're willing to reach out to the audience.

Stuffed Strongman

The Stuffed Stocking Strongman is a unique puppet design I came up with after high school. I was looking to create a puppet no one had seen before, and using stockings for facial features was something I'd only seen on dolls and mannequins.

I've never seen anyone build a puppet quite like the Strongman. The cool thing about this puppet is that he can be performed in a Bunraku style. Bunraku is an ancient Japanese puppetry technique that uses several puppeteers on each puppet to tell a story. Each puppeteer performs a part of the puppet to achieve a unified performance. There is a whole cast of characters performed in the same manner. Each character takes practice and teamwork, but you'll be amazed at the results. Everyone is helping the puppet along, but there is a force that gives the puppet a life and mind of its own. It's like magic when it all comes together.

Tools and Materials

Three pairs of panty hose (Q size)	White sheet foam	Spool of beige coat thread
Stuffing	Two white wooden beads	Scissors
Foam rubber	Two black pom-poms	Pencil or black permanent marker
Brown and black felt	Doll clothing	Glue
Square of fake fur	One long, dull needle	Pattern (page 75)

Using scissors and the pattern on page 75, cut out all the patterns from foam rubber. You should have an upper and a lower lip, two arms, two legs, and a head and upper torso piece.

1

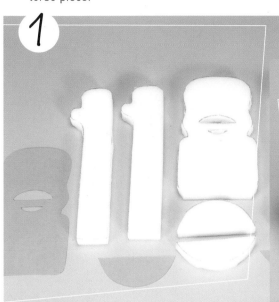

Using scissors, cut a finger slot in the back of both the upper and lower lip.

2

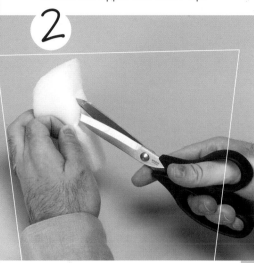

Glue the lips to the slots in the head and upper body foam rubber piece. The finger slots should be accessible through the slots in the head. For this puppet, the upper lip should be larger than the lower lip.

3

Professor Foaman's *travel tips*

If you use a marker to trace the pattern, cut away any black lines left from tracing on the foam rubber. The black lines will show through the panty hose.

4

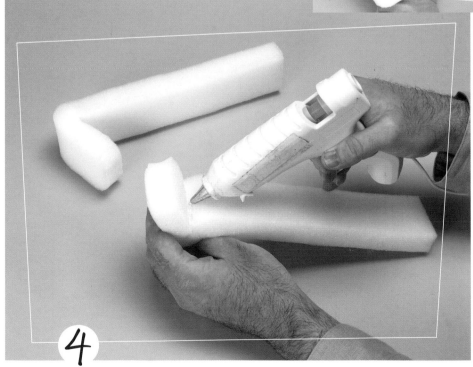

Create the feet by bending up the bottom 2" to 3" (5cm to 8cm) of the leg. Place a spot of glue in the bend to secure the shape of the feet.

Professor Foaman's
travel tips

If the limbs of the Strongman droop, use a spot of glue in the joint to give it support, or sew the limb into the position you want. You can also stitch the hands so they appear to grip.

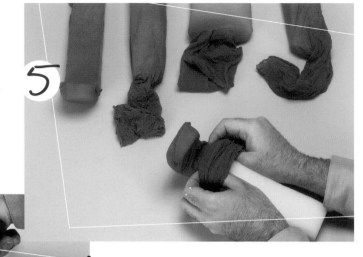

Cut the legs off all the panty hose, then pull the panty hose legs over the foam rubber head, legs and arms.

5

6 Use stuffing to give the face shape. Roll the stuffing into a ball and stuff it up the panty hose. Adjust the stuffing to get the shape you want. After you finish stuffing the back of the head where your hand will work the mouth, make two small cuts in the panty hose for the finger and thumb slots. You can use these cuts to help shape the stuffing.

Finish stuffing and shaping the head. All you need is a basic head shape at this point. Make sure there is no stuffing in the mouth.

7

Sew details in the face. Sew a stitch from one corner of the mouth to the other so the thread across the mouth helps maintain the shape. Next, work on the eyes. Push the needle from one eye socket to the other, then pinch the eye sockets under the stitch.

8

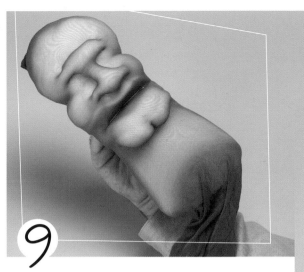

Fill in the body, belly and chest of the Strongman with stuffing. Shape the body once it has been stuffed. Tie off the bottom of the panty hose when you're happy with the shape of the body. Cut off the excess panty hose.

10

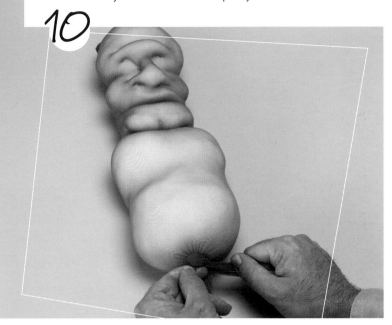

9

Create the nostrils by pinching up the bridge of the nose and drawing the needle through each nostril. Create eyebrows by drawing the needle through the upper eye to above the eyebrow. Then create a chin by drawing the needle and thread through the neck. Crisscross the needle and thread through these features, keeping the thread hidden in the pantyhose as much as possible. When you're satisfied with each feature, tie off the thread and trim the excess.

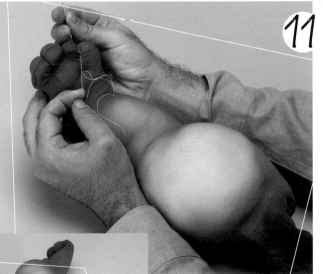

11 Stuff and shape the arms with stuffing. Draw the needle and thread through each finger to create extra definition. Stuff and shape the legs. Use the needle to add definition anywhere you like, and when you are satisfied with the arms and legs, tie off the panty hose and trim the excess.

12 Make sure the ends of the limbs are closed and the stuffing secure, then glue the arms and legs to the body.

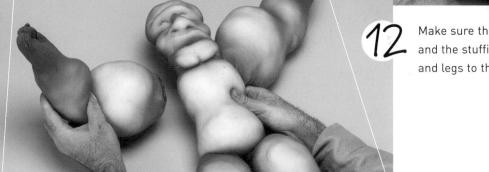

13

Add clothes to the Strongman, then assemble the face. Glue a small black pom-pom inside a white wooden bead for an eye, then glue the eyes in the eye socket. Add a little felt over the eyes for eyelids. Add fake fur hair to the head, trimming it until you are satisfied with the style, then glue it securely in place.

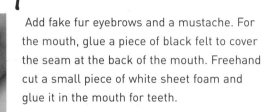

14

Add fake fur eyebrows and a mustache. For the mouth, glue a piece of black felt to cover the seam at the back of the mouth. Freehand cut a small piece of white sheet foam and glue it in the mouth for teeth.

Meet the Locals

Your "stuffed" puppet doesn't have to be a Strongman. What about making a Strongwoman, or a Grandmother, or a Sumo Wrestler? What will happen if the Sumo Wrestler takes the Strongwoman on a date, but his Grandmother ends up coming along too?

field guide to the Stuffed Strongman

The Strongman is good at barking out orders and showing off his muscles. He's got a knack for posing and flexing, so find the best poses. Use multiple puppeteers and have them practice hitting the poses on a verbal cue. When the Strongman says something, each puppeteer moves the puppet to position. The lead puppeteer should do the voice and guide the group. There should be a puppeteer performing the feet, another performing the arms, and the lead puppeteer performing the Strongman's head, mouth and hips. Give the Strongman some attitude and authority, and you never know what he might say.

Introduction

"Okay, everyone, let's get those wimpy bodies in shape. We're going to start out with some deep breathing exercises to get your heart pumping."

Big breath

"Spread your feet, open your arms wide and fill up those lungs. Ahh! Can you feel it?"

Left arm flex

"Now flex your left arm. Bring it up . . .(groan). . .and down. I am so huge!"

Right arm flex

"Flex your right arm. Bring it up. . . (groan). . .and down. . .(groan). Feel the burn! Feel it! We're working hard now! Push it."

Both arms flex

"Now raise them both! Don't be embarrassed that you're not as strong as me. Bring them up. . .(groan). . .and down. Okay, take a break. I know you can't keep up with me."

INSIDER tips

Have everyone shake the puppet a little bit while making the flex poses. This makes him look like he's really straining. If the lead puppeteer moans and groans while everyone's shaking, it will be even funnier. I know it's not in the tradition of the great Bunraku storytellers, but it's still entertaining.

Professor Foaman

For a long time I have called the basic shape for this puppet Foaman and decided he would live in a land called The Foaman Empire. When it came time to write this book, however, I needed to make a specific character. Professor Foaman was born. He became the perfect puppet to study Puppet Planet.

This is the only puppet for which I ever received a U.S. patent. It can be turned into any kind of character with a process so easy I felt it was worthy of claiming as my own. I found, after testing the project, that anyone can create puppet characters using the basic Foaman shape. I'm hoping that Professor Foaman and his Foaman Kit will be the next big thing.

Tools and Materials

5" x 6" x 12" (13cm x 15cm x 30cm) block of foam (this amount creates two puppets)

1" (3cm) thin foam square

Coat hanger

Red and white felt

Long shag white fur

Black rimmed glasses

Clip-on tie

White posterboard

Two large circle bubble stickers

Pliers with wire cutters

Electric carving knife

Scissors

Black permanent marker

Needle and white thread

Dremel tool (optional)

Mid-grade sandpaper (optional)

Glue

Eye template (page 13)

Patterns (page 76)

Trace the head pattern, found on page 76, on the foam block and the hand pattern on the foam square. Trace the pattern on both sides of the foam block. Cut out both the hand and the head using an electric knife. Line up your cuts on both sides of the foam block. When finished, you should have two hands and two head pieces. Set aside one of the head pieces for a future puppet.

Fold the puppet head in half, then use one blade of the scissors to gently open a large enough space for your thumb and fingers in the back of the foam block. The finger slot should go into the larger, upper portion of the head, and the thumb slot into the smaller, lower chin section. Make sure not to cut a hole through the foam.

Freehand draw the basic shape and outline of the Professor's face on the foam. When done, cut out the basic shape using the electric knife. Don't worry if your puppet isn't perfect right now. All you need is a basic shape.

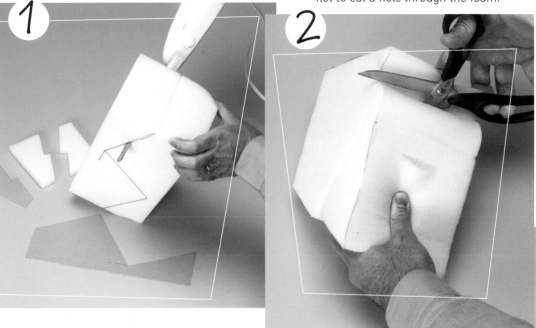

Draw the details of the face. Focus on the chin, mouth and nose, but not the eyes since this puppet's eyes are on his glasses. You can use the mouth pattern to help create the mouth.

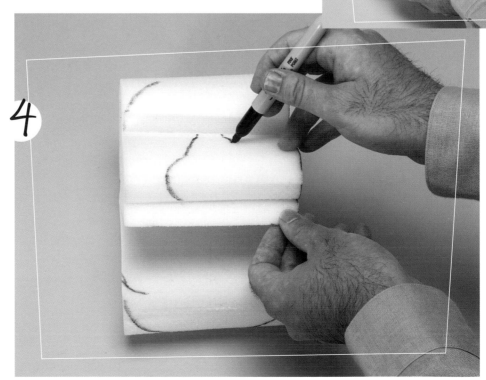

Begin trimming away the foam from the face. Use the electric knife to trim away the outside areas of the face, then use the scissors to cut straight into the foam to create the nose. Make your cuts straight, otherwise the foam will lose its shape. The deeper you cut, the bigger your nose will be. Save the foam scraps to make the ears.

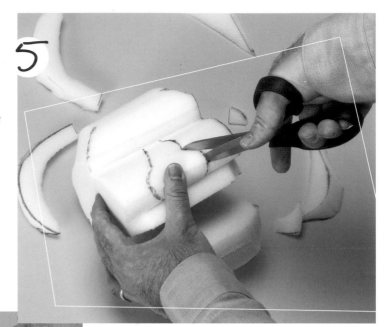

Cut away the sides of the nose with your scissors. Push the point of the scissors all the way to the edge of the nose, where you made your straight cut in the last step, before cutting away the foam.

Round, or bevel, the edges of the face by digging the scissors into the foam and snipping away the sharp edges. This should remove all the dark marker lines. Once the edges are rounded, smooth the foam if you like, following the directions on page 14.

Use the pattern on page 76 to cut out the white felt front and back body and the red felt mouth. Create an arm with a 10" x 5" (25cm x 13cm) piece of white felt. Create a cuff in the arms by sewing a 1" (3cm) hem, leaving the ends open. This will create a loop in the cuff. Roll the arm and sew the seam closed, leaving the last 2" (5cm) near the cuff open. Turn the arm right side out to hide the seam. Do this for both arms. Position the arms inside the body, folding the ends of the arms down. Cover the arms with the front of the body, then sew the left and right edges of the body, attaching the arms to the body. Make sure to sew only the shoulders of the arm. Turn the body right side out so the arms are on the outside.

Glue the red felt in the mouth. When you do so, fold the mouth and glue the felt in the folded mouth, otherwise the felt will bunch when the mouth is closed.

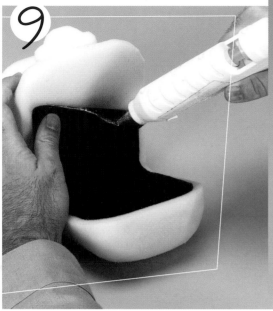

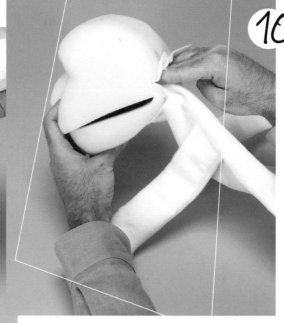

Attach the small tab on the front of the body into the thumb slot, and attach the large tab on the back of the body into the slot for the fingers in the upper head. Carefully add glue to the slots to keep the body secure. Make sure not to glue the slots closed so your fingers can still operate the mouth.

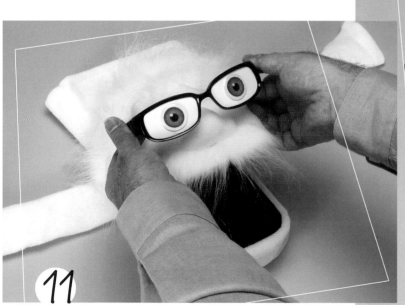

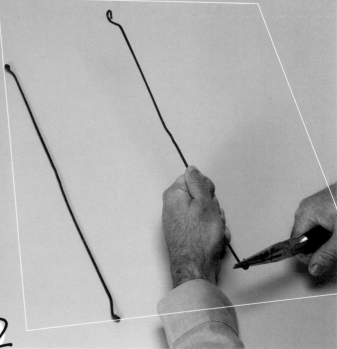

Create the face. Cut a strip of white shag fur for the mustache, smaller strips for bushy eyebrows, and a patch for the hair. Glue the fur on the head. Use scraps of foam to cut a thin, half-moon shape for each ear. Glue the ears on either side of the head. Follow the directions on page 13 to create eyes. Prepare the glasses by taking the lenses out of a pair of sunglasses. Fill the lens area with posterboard and attach the eyes to the posterboard. Place the glasses on the head and secure them with glue at the ears.

Create the arm rods from a coat hanger. Cut the top of the coat hanger away, and then cut halfway between the bottom bends in the hanger. Straighten both sides of the coat hanger and bend the ends of both wires into loops using pliers, hiding any sharp ends of the wires.

Glue a clip-on tie under the chin. Push an arm rod **13** through the slot in the cuff of each sleeve. Bend the end of the rod through the cuff, then place the hand in the bend. Close the bend, trapping the hand in place, then use glue to secure. Do this for both hands.

Meet the Locals

The basic Foaman shape can be adapted to a multitude of characters, making it easy to create a spontaneous puppet show. One puppet's words and actions can lead to the next until you've come up with an entire show. It's a great project for schools, groups and clubs because you get to be an artist, a writer and an actor all in one afternoon. You could even workshop an idea that can eventually be a finished play that you could tour with to other locations.

field guide to Professor Foaman

Professor Foaman is a mouth puppet, so he's great for speaking. You'll want to practice his arm moves to get as comfortable as you can with Foaman so you can focus on the dialogue while performing.

Most of the time you will want to keep the hands of Professor Foaman at rest on his stomach, but adding a gesture here and there to make a point is a nice way to make Foaman seem even more real. Try mouthing the words to a song with Foaman while the puppet claps to the beat, or have him point at the people he is talking to. You can practice these moves and see what he looks like to others by working in front of a mirror.

Foaman giving a hug

"Welcome to my Puppet Planet laboratory. I'm so glad you could join me today."

Foaman arguing

"I disagree. You certainly can conquer the Stuffed Strongman. It's a simple process of mind over matter!"

Foaman clapping

"Congratulations, students! You've done a wonderful job."

Podium President

I realized you could make a good living being a puppeteer when I was in college. An agency I worked for sold puppets to companies for entertaining their employees at yearly meetings. The puppets were custom-made to resemble the CEO, and I performed them in a spoof during the meeting. Pretty soon I was all over the country performing with executive caricatures. Performing was easy because I could hide behind a podium with a microphone and have the puppet above my head. It looked just like the caricature was standing at the podium. It always got a big laugh and the executives would marvel at their puppet likenesses. This time I made my own likeness, since I'm the president of my own planet. President Kennedy has a nice ring to it, I think.

Tools and Materials

1" (3cm) foam rubber	Red fabric	Drill	Contact cement (Weldwood was used for this puppet)
White plastic bottle	Flesh-colored fabric	Long, dull needle	
White tube socks	Scrap fabric	Needle and white thread	Matching gloves (optional)
Rubber baby bottle nipples	Size 5 boy's suit with shirt, tie, sport coat and slacks	Straight pins	Patterns (page 77)
Stuffing	Eye clasps	Pen or pencil	
Square of fake fur (hair colored)	Reference photo (of the subject)	Foam brush	
		Scissors	

Using scissors and the patterns on page 77, cut out the head and body from foam rubber. You will need two pieces for the body and two for the head.

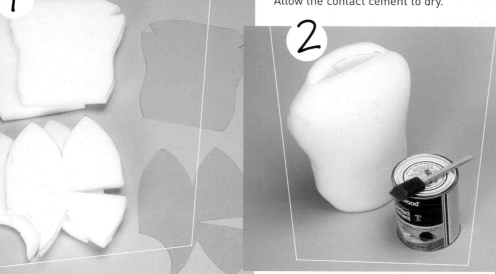

1

Following the directions on the contact cement, glue the body and head together. Glue all sides of the body except the flat top part and the bottom. Line up the mouth notches on the head, then press the front of the head together. Do not glue the back of the head or the mouth closed yet. Allow the contact cement to dry.

2

Using scrap foam, cut a 4" x 2" (10cm x 5cm) strip and a 2" x 4" (5cm x 10cm) half circle. Using contact cement, glue the half circle below the mouth. Glue the flat strip above the mouth. Both of these pieces need to be solidly attached because they operate the mouth. Allow the contact cement to dry.

3

Professor Foaman's *travel tips*

Make sure you use contact cement only in a well-ventilated area and avoid skin contact.

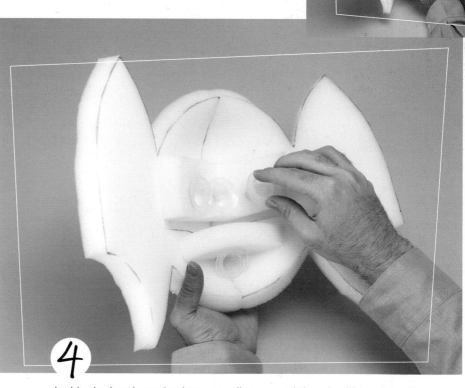

4

Inside the head, mark where your fingers and thumb will be placed to operate the puppet's mouth. You will be sticking your fingers into the strip and your thumb under the half circle foam piece. On the marks, cut into the foam rubber, but not all the way through. Insert the rubber nipples into the cuts and under the foam half circle, using contact cement to secure them in place. The baby bottle nipples will help you operate the mouth.

Professor Foaman's
travel tips

If you have trouble getting the fabric to cover the head without wrinkling, you can use a slightly larger version of the head pattern to cover the foam head. Sew the head pieces together, adding extra material to the neck.

Cut out the mouth pattern from red fabric. Place the red fabric into the mouth, pushing the tabs on either side to the interior of the head. Line up the fabric edge with the edge of the mouth, then use contact cement to secure it in place. Glue the side tabs in the interior. Cut more strips of scrap fabric and glue them over the rubber nipples. Once the fabric is dry, cut finger and thumb holes in the fabric.

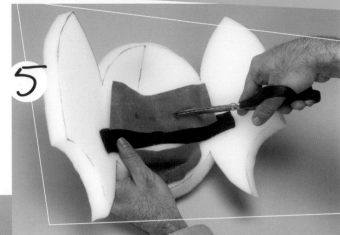

5

6

Use contact cement to finish gluing the head pieces together.

Stretch the flesh-colored fabric over the head and hand sew it, from the back of the head, in place. Avoid wrinkles in the fabric. See page 15 for more information on sewing. Trim the fabric, leaving enough hanging down over the head to attach it to the body. Don't worry that the mouth is covered at this point.

7

Trim the socks to the size you want for the arms of the puppet. For this body, that will be about 8" (20cm). Fill the socks with stuffing and attach them to the body with glue, gluing around the open end of the sock. Attach the head, pulling the extra neck fabric through the neck of the body and gluing it to the inside of the body. If necessary, trim the excess neck material.

8

Create the eyes by cutting an eye shape from a white plastic bottle. Turn the shape over, retrace it on the white plastic bottle and cut out a second eye shape. Drill holes in the plastic for the eyes, and push the eye posts into the holes. Take a strip of the fabric you used for the head and create eyelids. Trim the eyelids to fit, wrapping the lid around the edge of the eye. Use contact cement to secure the eyelids.

9

Carefully cut open the mouth of the puppet. Fold the edges of the mouth in and glue them against the foam inside the mouth.

10

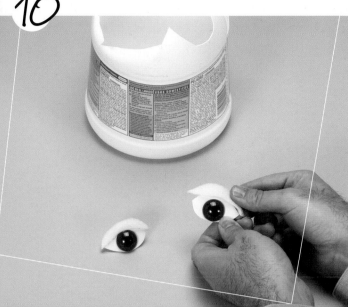

Professor Foaman's *travel tips*

Getting good photos of the person you are basing your puppet on is crucial to capturing a likeness. Use a front view and profile shots of the person. If the performance is to be a surprise, you may have to be creative in how you get the photos. For example, tell the person the photos are part of a scrapbook project.

11

Use a reference photo to design the face. Roll some flesh-colored fabric into a nose and glue it on the face, adjusting the fabric as needed. Next, add the eyes above the nose, adjusting them until you're satisfied. Secure the eyes by making slits in the fabric and clasping them in place. Next, use fur to add eyebrows above the eyes, and then hair, sewing or gluing the fur in place. Finally, add ears by rolling another piece of flesh-colored fabric and gluing it to either side of the face.

Professor Foaman's
travel tips

You may want to wear gloves that match the skin color of the puppet. For a more realistic look, use the same material as the puppet or dye white gloves to match.

70

Dress the puppet. Start with a shirt, then add the jacket and tie. Add stuffing to the sleeve of one arm and pin the end of the sleeve to the side of the jacket, so it appears the hand is inside the jacket pocket.

12

13

Roll up the cuff of the other arm. Cut the leg off a pair of pants the same color as the suit. Pin the middle of the leg to the rolled cuff of the arm. Insert your arm into the pant's leg, making sure your arm looks natural in the suit. Make adjustments as necessary, for example, shortening the pant's leg. Once you are satisfied, sew or glue the pant leg to the rolled cuff of the suit.

Meet the Locals

Local heroes make good podium puppets as well. What better way to celebrate them than to re-enact their heroic deeds with a puppet-likeness at a ceremony held in their honor. You could then take their routine to local schools to demonstrate the important role they serve in the community.

field guide to the Podium President

This puppet can be made to resemble virtually anyone in your community. This means that no one is safe from becoming the next Podium President. Teachers, doctors, family members—they are all potential entertainment for the next meeting or gathering. All you need is a podium, scripted material and the puppet. The project works best when it's a surprise. It's also important that it's done in good taste and with good intentions. Try to capture the fun parts of the subject's personality and you'll entertain everyone, including the subject.

Presidential wave

"Welcome, everyone, to this week's monthly meeting. I. . .uh. Wait a minute. I mean. . .Oh no! I've got puppet meeting mania!"

Thumbs up

"I want to tell everyone that sales are way up. And so is the hand that's up my . . .Oops. Anyway. . ."

Making a point

"The point is we need to sell more books. Now, who's in charge of this two-bit operation? Oh. . .me? Okay, great, the meeting's over."

Performance Workshop

You may find that more coverage will be needed to hide the puppeteer. Use black fabric taped to two microphone or music stands to add extra wings to the podium, for example. Think about entering and exiting the podium as well. Hiding behind a podium for any length of time can be uncomfortable. If you can, position the podium next to a large piece of furniture or a wall. You may need to escape if the speaker before or after you has a lengthy speech to deliver.

INSIDER tips

The point at which the puppeteer's coat sleeve meets the puppet's coat sleeve should appear to be the elbow joint of the puppet. To enforce this idea you'll want to keep a constant bend in the elbow by tucking your arm in close to the puppet's body. This way you can gesture up and out without showing the bottom part of your sleeve.

Patterns

Enlarge these patterns to 200%.

Rod and Reel Rodent, page 18

TWO TAN SHEET
FOAM EYES

TWO TAN SHEET FOAM EARS
AND TWO BROWN FUR EARS

TAN SHEET FOAM TAIL

Spoon Balloon Frog, page 22

ONE GREEN SHEET FOAM FROG

Pillow Buddy, page 30

TWO BLACK FELT
EYELASHES

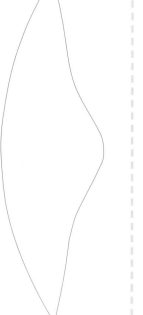

BLACK FELT MOUTH

Sweatshirt Sheep, page 42

FOUR SWEATSHIRT LEGS

TWO SWEATSHIRT
EARS

Crafty Cockatoo, page 34

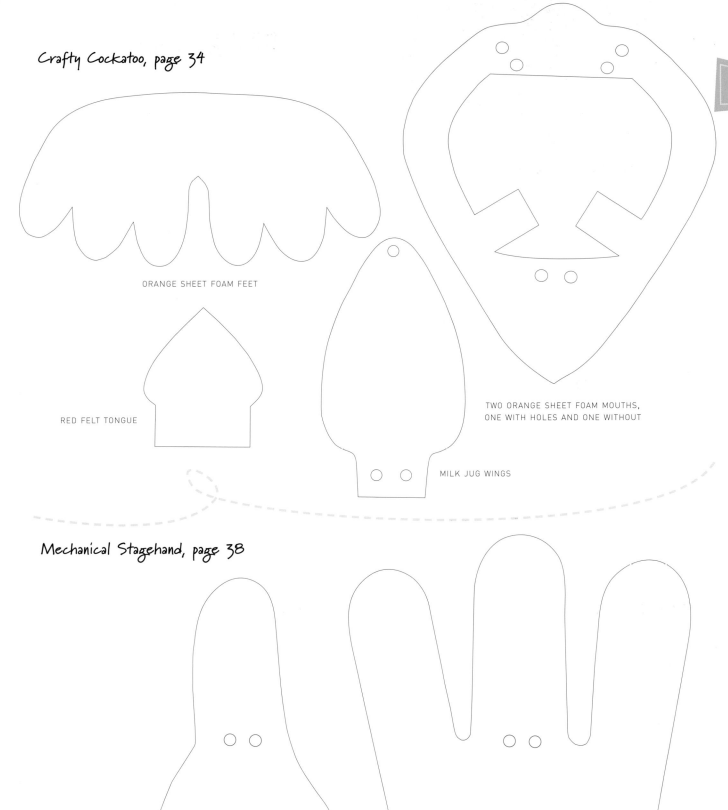

ORANGE SHEET FOAM FEET

RED FELT TONGUE

TWO ORANGE SHEET FOAM MOUTHS,
ONE WITH HOLES AND ONE WITHOUT

MILK JUG WINGS

Mechanical Stagehand, page 38

HARD PLASTIC THUMB

HARD PLASTIC FINGERS

Enlarge these patterns to 200%,
and enlarge again at 125% to bring to full size.

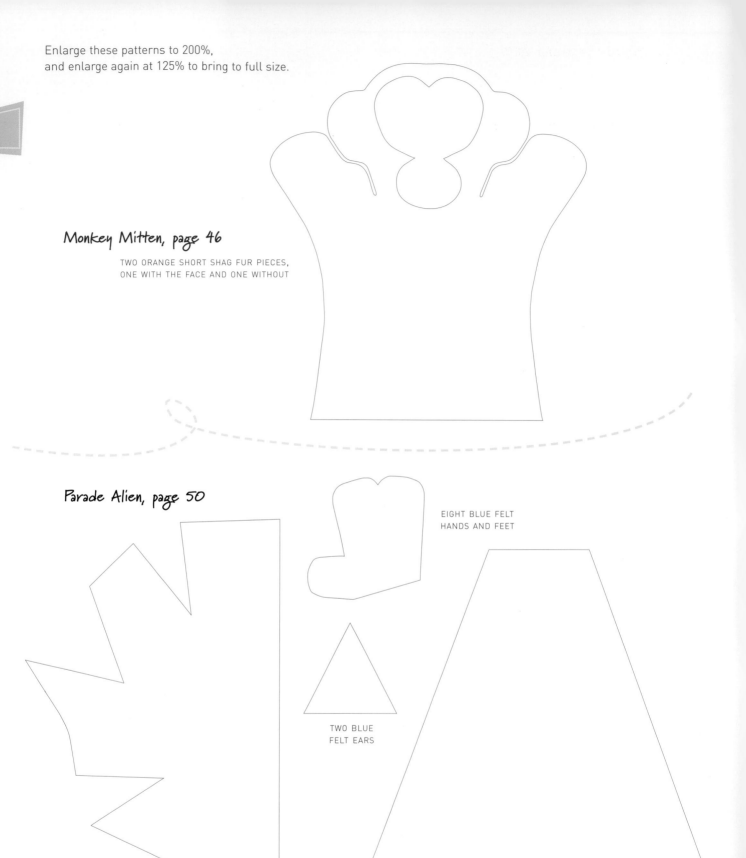

Monkey Mitten, page 46

TWO ORANGE SHORT SHAG FUR PIECES,
ONE WITH THE FACE AND ONE WITHOUT

Parade Alien, page 50

EIGHT BLUE FELT
HANDS AND FEET

TWO BLUE
FELT EARS

TWO BLUE FELT
HEAD PIECES

TWO ORANGE FELT ARMS AND ONE ORANGE FELT BODY

Enlarge these patterns to 200%.

Stuffed Strongman, page 54

FOAM RUBBER UPPER LIP

FOAM RUBBER LOWER LIP

FOAM RUBBER ARM

FOAM RUBBER ARM

FOAM RUBBER HEAD AND TORSO

Enlarge these patterns to 200%,
and enlarge again at 125% to bring to full size.

Professor Foaman, page 60

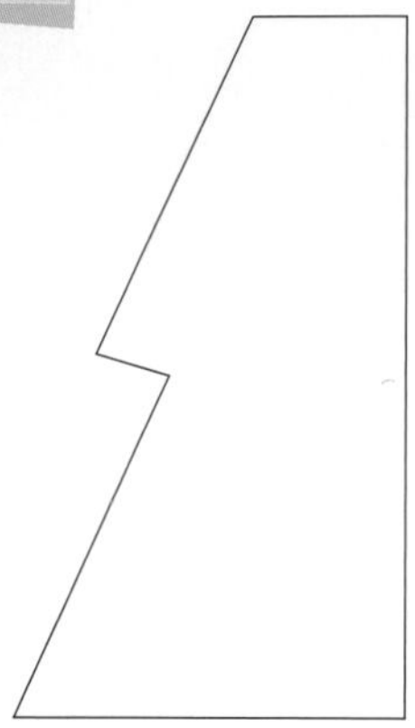

THIN FOAM RUBBER HAND

WHITE FELT FRONT BODY

RED FELT MOUTH

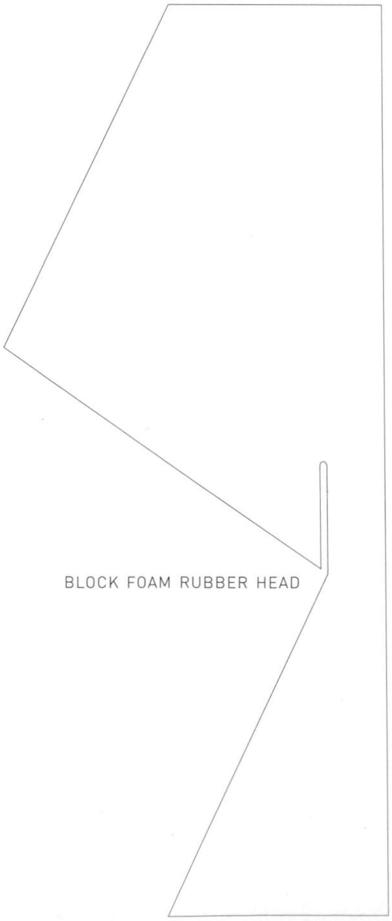

WHITE FELT
BACK BODY

BLOCK FOAM RUBBER HEAD

Enlarge these patterns to 200%.

Podium President, page 66

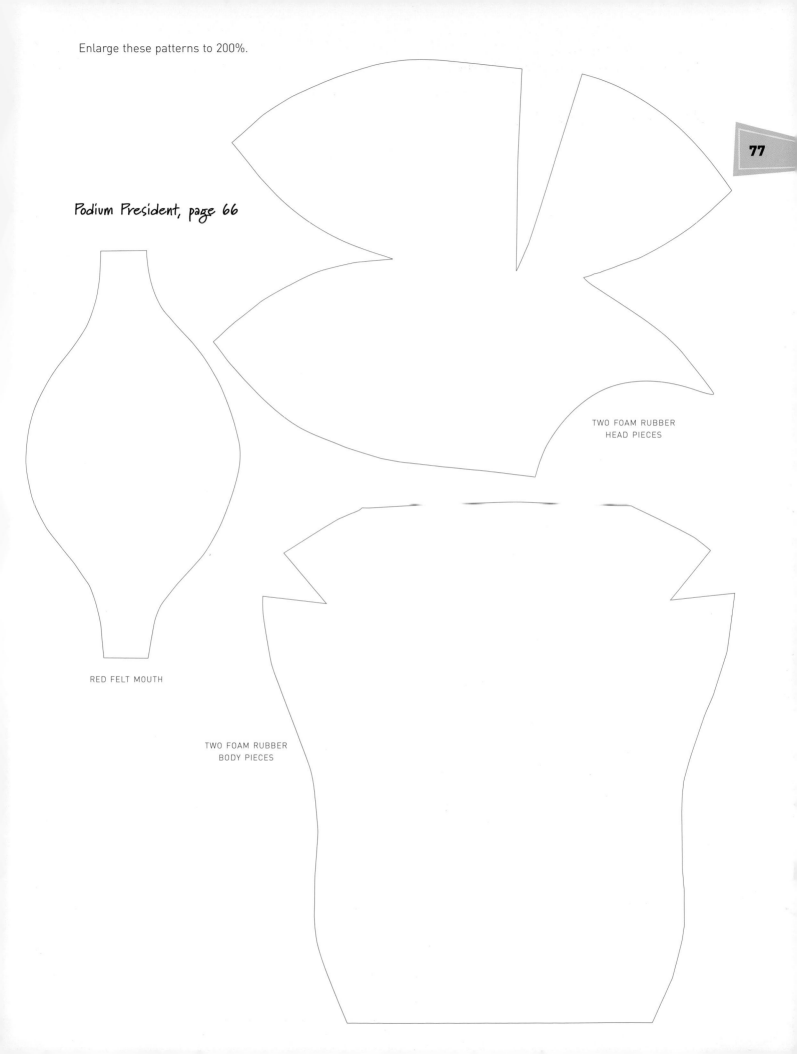

TWO FOAM RUBBER
HEAD PIECES

RED FELT MOUTH

TWO FOAM RUBBER
BODY PIECES

Resources

Most of the materials used in this book can be found at your local arts and crafts store or fabric stores. For specialty materials, you may want to try the following sources. If you have any questions about the supplies used in this book, look for the manufacturer's contact information.

Supplies

American Art Clay Co., Inc. (AMACO)
1-800-374-1600
www.amaco.com
Polymer clay and supplies

Dazian, LLC
1-877-232-9426
www.dazian.com
Fabrics, including Fosshape, a lightweight fabric that can be heat-activated to maintain its shape

FX Warehouse, Inc.
1-386-254-0497
www.fxwarehouseinc.com
Online ordering and free how-to guides for FX artists and scenic studios

Smooth-On, Inc.
1-800-762-0744
www.smooth-on.com
Liquid rubber, plastic, molding and casting supplies

Associations

Puppeteers of America
P.O. Box 330
West Liberty, IA 52778
1-888-568-6235
www.puppeteers.org
National nonprofit organization of people who love puppet theater

Index

Take a creative journey with North Light

In **Puppet Mania!**, John Kennedy's first book, you'll use easy-to-find materials to make 13 delightful, original and zany puppets such as the Running Rabbit, Banana Buddy, Sock Puppy and the Boxing Kangaroo. A technique section, information on bringing the puppet to life and plenty of variation ideas make this the perfect book for anyone who wants to start making their own puppets today!

ISBN 1-58180-372-9
ISBN-13 978-1-58180-372-3
Paperback   128 pages   32386

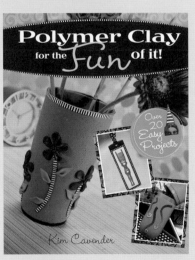

As every polymer person knows, working with polymer clay is all about having fun and making great stuff. With its over 20 bright and colorful projects and variations, **Polymer Clay for the Fun of It!** shows readers how to have a good time with polymer clay. The book gives readers a comprehensive and lighthearted polymer clay "primer" along with a detailed techniques section to make getting started fun and easy. As a bonus feature, readers get "Just for the fun of it..." tips to keep them inspired. Each project begins with an often tongue-in-cheek quote that matches the easygoing tone of the book. **Kim Cavender** shows you how you can throw all of the rules out the window and just, well, have fun!

ISBN 1-58180-684-1
ISBN-13 978-1-58180-684-7
paperback   128 pages   33320

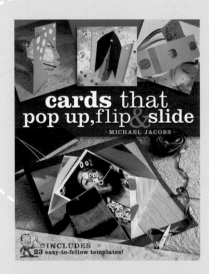

In **Cards that Pop up, Flip & Slide** you'll learn how to craft one-of-a-kind greetings with moving parts such as pop-ups, sliders and flaps. Choose from 22 step-by-step projects that use a variety of papers—from handmade and printed to recycled—to create unique graphic looks. You'll also learn how to create coordinating envelopes to complete the look of your card. **Michael Jacobs** inspires you to jazz up all of your cards with the fun and easy techniques in this book, including using inks, collage and colored pencils in fresh new ways.

ISBN 1-58180-596-9
ISBN-13 978-1-58180-596-3
paperback   96 pages   33109